1991 EDITION

Job Search 101

By Brian Jud

Designed by
Ellen Gregory

First Edition
Published by Marketing Directions, Inc.

Copyright © 1991, by Brian Jud
First Edition - Second Printing
Published by Marketing Directions, Inc.
P. O. Box 715, Avon, CT 06001

Other books by the author:

The Career Action Plan
The College Action Plan

ISBN 1-880218-00-3

Library of Congress Catalog Card Number: 91-75075

Table of Contents

Page

Chapter One - The Way A Job Search <u>Should</u> Work   1
• The importance of planning • The three phases of a job search

Chapter Two - What Do You Have to Offer An Employer?   7
• Features, advantages and benefits • How to assess benefits • How to quantify and qualify your benefits • Product definition • Continuing education • The proper image • Physical and mental conditioning • Evaluating your competition • Appearance • Maintaining a positive attitude • Career Killers • Assessing your strengths and weaknesses • Creating your Brain Trust

Chapter Three - How to be in the Right Place At the Right Time   24
• Determining where to best sell your services • Physical location • International opportunities • Domestic opportunities • Going direct • Using middlemen (personnel agencies, temporary assignments, personnel consultants, state agencies, college staff)

Chapter Four - How To Determine Your Market Price   31
• Establishing value for your services • <u>External Factors</u> (market conditions, psychological factors, wage standards) • <u>Internal Factors</u> (costs, distinctiveness, geographic location, education, psychic income, special skills) • Monthly cash-flow analysis • Pricing formula

Chapter Five - <u>PASS</u> The Word About Your Availability   39
• Communications strategy • The communications mix • The Seven Cs • <u>Publicity</u> (testimonials, references, published articles, support groups, associations, press kit) • <u>Ad</u>vertising (cover letters, resumes, audio resumes, video resumes, follow-up letters, narrowcasting, rejection-response letters, miscellaneous letters) • <u>Sales Promotion</u> (reply cards, personal cards, advance cards, sampling, literature) • <u>S</u>elling (networking, telephone skills, job fairs, trade shows)

Chapter Six - Prospecting For Golden Opportunities   83
• <u>Establishing criteria</u> (company characteristics, ideal description for your job) • Sources of information (newspapers, magazines, directories, trade shows, job fairs, personal contacts, agencies, personal observation) • Qualify and Prioritize

Chapter Seven - Creating Your Job-Search Plan   92
• The Mission Statement • Objectives • Monthly, weekly and daily plans • Creating your job-search plan

Chapter Eight - The Early Stages of the Interviewing Process   101
• The importance of practicing • Types of interviews • Atypical situations • Reasons to interview • The interview life cycle • The sequence of interviews • Stage One: Preparation • Stage Two: Introduction

Chapter Nine - The Interview: Making Your Presentation   118
• The response technique • Stage Three: Presentation • SALARY • Beginning your presentation • Support statements • Proof statements • Handling skepticism • Handling objections • 75 Questions interviewers will ask you

Chapter Ten - Interview The Interviewer   **129**
• Stage Four: Accumulation • How to ask questions • Types of questions
• 65 questions you can ask an interviewer • Stage Five: Conclusion • When to ask
for commitment • How to ask for commitment • Direct techniques • Indirect
techniques • Actively listen

Chapter Eleven - What's Going Right (and Wrong) In Your Job Search   **142**
• Why perform the evaluation • What to evaluate • How to perform the
evaluation • Career-Progress Checklist • Post-Interview Checklist

Chapter Twelve - Play "20 Questions" To Stimulate Your Creativity   **150**
• Brainstorming • Twenty techniques and questions to help stimulate your thinking

Chapter Thirteen - Stop The World, I Want To Get On.   **164**
• How to take ACTION • Negotiating the offer • Accepting the
offer • Declining the offer • The rescinded offer

Exhibits

1	The Funnel for Career Success	3
2	Talent-Analysis Sheet	9
3	Talent-Analysis Sheet for Education	11
4	Self-Analysis Balance Sheet	19
5	Channels of Distribution	26
6	Sample Letter for Temporary Position	27
7	Monthly Cash-Flow Analysis	35
8	Word Finders	49
9	Sample Cover Letter	50
10	Sample Cover Letter	51
11	Resume Structure For The Employment Segment	56
12	Resume Structure For The Education Segment	57
13	Cover-Letter/Resume Checklist	61
14	Format for Tracking Contacts	66
15	First Follow-Up Letter	66
16	Rejection-Response Letter	67
17	Narrowcast Letter	70
18	Copy For Personal Reply Card	73
19	Copy For Personal Career Card	74
20	Trade-Show Handout	81
21	Typical Monthly Plan	94
22	Typical Daily Plan	95
23	Outline For Your Job-Search Plan	97
24	Technique for Responding to Questions	119
25	Questions Interviewers Will Ask You	126
26	Questions You Can Ask an Interviewer	132
27	Sample Career-Progress Checklist	145
28	Sample Post-Interview Checklist	146

CHAPTER ONE

The Way A Job Search <u>Should</u> Work

Many books have been written about how to get a job, but this one is different for one major reason. It is a practical guide for creating your own customized job-search campaign, written by someone who has been on both sides of the interviewing desk. It offers creative ideas for you to use in your quest, as well as new ways to implement the more traditional job-search techniques.

Unique in its approach.

<u>Job Search 101</u> is actually written from three different perspectives. First, it is written from the viewpoint of a person who has been through what you are going through. I have experienced the frustrations, apprehensions and feelings of dejection and elation that come with a job search.

I understand your position and apprehension, whether you're a recent college graduate or a forty-three year old "displaced" person seeking a new career. I've been fired and fired-up. I've been over-employed, under-employed, self-employed and unemployed. I've had to seek full-time employment while going to night school, working part-time on weekends and at the same time supporting a family of four.

Secondly, I've been on the other side of the desk. I have reviewed thousands of resumes and conducted hundreds of interviews. I have witnessed many different interviewing and communicating techniques used by people applying for positions ranging from secretarial to management.

And from the third viewpoint, I have over 20 years of marketing experience, developing products and bringing them successfully to the marketplace. <u>Job Search 101</u> essentially takes these marketing skills and translates them into the terminology of the job search. The combination of all this experience assures an empathetic yet strategic focus on the efforts you must make to achieve the goals that you have determined are important to you.

It's as easy as PIE.

Many people have written that there is no formula for success in a job-search campaign. There actually is a formula, and if you follow it, there is no doubt that you will create a new job for yourself in less time than you otherwise would have.

The formula for success:

SUCCESS = HARD WORK

In order to achieve success, you have to put a great deal of effort into your search. If you do that, positive results will be forthcoming. And you'll be even more successful if you organize your work, so that it is directed toward accomplishments. This overall design is simple, and all it takes is planning, implementation and evaluation. You can remember that with one acronym: **PIE.**

1) **P**lan. If you begin by planning where you want to go, the trip there will be shorter. The essence of Job Search 101 is to plan your trip before you set out on it.

2) Implement. Once you have outlined your objectives, strategies and tactics, you must immediately put them in action. Use professional creativity, and you'll see results quickly.

3) Evaluate. You can work very hard and still not experience success if you are working on the wrong activities, or performing them incorrectly. Therefore, you must determine if your actions are taking you closer to your objectives, and if not, why not. Then you make corrections.

Avoid the "Ready, Fire, Aim" perspective.

The concept of planning your efforts before you proceed with any implementation step is fundamental to your success. It is vital to create a plan for the activities which you are about to undertake. Those who lack a plan will probably end up getting a "job," but it will most likely take longer and not be the best one that they might have had.

You can think of Job Search 101 as a road map for your journey to career success. For example, when you begin planning any trip, you start with the knowledge of where you are and where you want to go. Then you investigate the various routes to get there before deciding which one you will take (creating your plan). And then you begin your journey (implementing your plan). You check your progress periodically against certain landmarks you have established in order to confirm that you are going in the right direction (evaluating your plan). If you're "on the right path," you continue along as you had originally planned and reach your destination in the most efficient way. If not, you consult your map to find out where you went wrong and then correct your mistake by getting back on the correct route.

You may even come to a dead end. Of course you didn't plan to be there, but some unforeseen event occurred that led you unknowingly to it. Now you have to take some action to find out where you took the wrong turn and get back on track. Hopefully, once you've planned your trip and followed directions, you'll reach your destination without any trouble.

The function of Job Search 101 is to help you prepare your "roadmap" to career success. In it, you'll learn how to recognize detour signs, avoid stop signs, locate efficient shortcuts, minimize tolls and plan to take the best route to reach your destination in the least amount of time. Your plan is the map that you will create in order to lead yourself, step by step, to your final objective.

Funnelling your activities.

Exhibit 1 presents a summary of the actions you will need to create and perform in your quest for a satisfying career. The "Funnel For Career Success" graphically depicts how the many parts of a career search must blend together to attain your final objective. All the ingredients must be present for success to occur. Your job search will take a great deal of time and effort, but the results will be extremely rewarding.

EXHIBIT 1: THE FUNNEL FOR CAREER SUCCESS

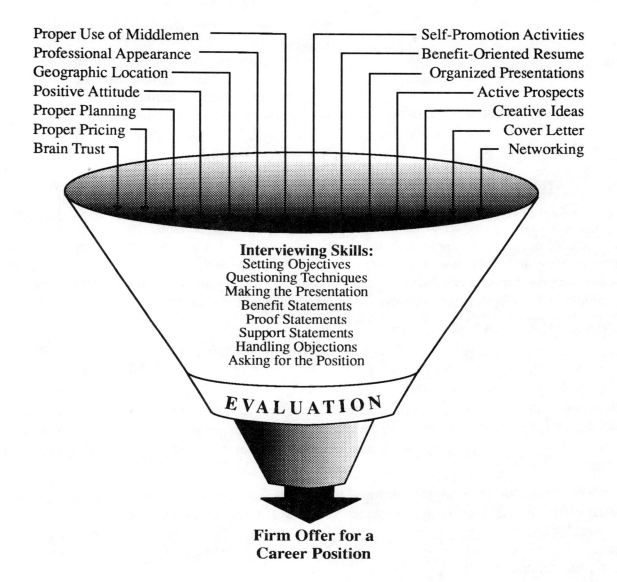

Proper Use of Middlemen
Professional Appearance
Geographic Location
Positive Attitude
Proper Planning
Proper Pricing
Brain Trust

Self-Promotion Activities
Benefit-Oriented Resume
Organized Presentations
Active Prospects
Creative Ideas
Cover Letter
Networking

Interviewing Skills:
Setting Objectives
Questioning Techniques
Making the Presentation
Benefit Statements
Proof Statements
Support Statements
Handling Objections
Asking for the Position

EVALUATION

**Firm Offer for a
Career Position**

The size of the opening of the funnel will be determined by the length of time you have available for your quest. If you have sufficient time to search for a position, the opening at the top of the funnel will be narrow. You can more accurately target your prospects, and be more critical of the opportunities that result.

Conversely, if you don't have a significant amount of time, you can view the top of the funnel to be much wider, providing many more names of prospective employers and more interviews in a shorter amount of time. The techniques presented in the following chapters allow you to create the appropriate funnel size for your specific circumstances.

THE THREE PHASES OF A JOB SEARCH.

INVESTIGATION

CREATION

IMPLEMENTATION
▼
EVALUATION
▼
AFFIRMATION

DESTINATION

Regardless of the time allowed for your search, your activities should be performed in proper and logical order to be most effective. The illustration to the left graphically depicts this sequence of events. Each step must be performed before the next is undertaken. These steps occur in three separate stages over the period of time you have allowed.

The first occurs before the interview itself, when you are evaluating yourself and your opportunities, and preparing and sending your correspondence. The second phase happens during the interview and includes all the techniques you can use to obtain an offer for the position you want. And the third is an evaluation period, during which you must step back to gauge your progress and make necessary corrections in order to achieve the job offer.

PHASE ONE: PLANNING

Before any work can be started, you must perform research into what you have to offer, what you want to do, where you want to do it and for what price. Then you manipulate all this information into a cohesive plan that will properly direct your efforts.

Once you have completed this, you have to find out what new opportunities are available as a result of your revised plan and seek them out. This includes prospecting to find the potential employers, performing research on them to develop adequate information and contacting them to arrange an interview.

While you are doing all that, you also have to create your cover-letter/resume package and a wide variety of additional correspondence. You have to write follow-up letters, rejection-response letters, and announcements. You will learn to plan and implement a customized job search that will promote you as a professional candidate, more qualified for a given position than are your competitors.

A critical element in this first phase is to learn interviewing skills and practice them until you are expert in their application. You should practice asking and answering questions, making presentations, handling objections, listening, eye communication and even shaking hands with people. The more you practice without any stress, the more effective you will be when the pressure is on.

PHASE TWO: IMPLEMENTATION

During phase two you are actually on the interview. You must utilize all your skills of listening and persuasion in order to bring the interview to a successful conclusion. Most interviewees simply "attend" an interview. They obviously know their background, and they wait to be asked questions so they may describe previous experience and education. "Attending" an interview comes across as a re-reading of the applicant's resume, with a few embellishments.

Conversely, there is the situation in which the interviewee thinks he should aggressively control the interview and exhibit a strong personality. According to this theory, the interviewer is viewed as the passive party, with the applicant directing the areas and topics of discussion.

These scenarios represent the two extremes, and neither should be considered the proper interviewing strategy. The interview should be viewed as a mutual exchange that provides both parties with the information they need in order to make the decision to create a long-term, mutually beneficial relationship. This can only occur with active participation on the parts of both people.

PHASE THREE: EVALUATION

The evaluation phase helps you determine if your actions are taking you in the proper direction. Major corrections may be necessary, or you may need to do some fine tuning only. In this stage you'll provide the feedback required to assess your progress. As you well know, activity in itself does not always equal accomplishment. You may find yourself busy at doing something but not bringing yourself closer to your goal. You must determine if your actions are achieving your objectives or taking you in a different direction. If they are, what can you do to change it?

The master chef with a master plan.

You can view all these phases of your quest as you would the ingredients in a recipe. If you leave out an important part, the end result will probably not taste the way you wanted it to. Similarly, you have to create your own career recipe with its overall plan that serves as the list of ingredients and instructions for mixing them together.

The four major "food groups" in your recipe are price, place, product and promotion. These are called the "Four Ps" of marketing, and represent the major categories that must be manipulated to introduce or maintain a product successfully.

From this point on, you will be the marketing manager for your job search, marketing your "former self" as a product. Your initial task is to research your product and create a plan to market it most successfully in whatever field you have chosen. In a career sense, you will objectively assess your strengths and weaknesses to determine what you have to do to make them more marketable and profitable. You must determine what and where your target market will be, what its needs are and how your product's benefits can satisfy those needs.

You will price your new product based on the total value that you can bring to a prospective employer. And you must determine the market "place," which refers to the geographical location in which you wish to live, as well as the various methods of distribution available to you (i.e., employment agencies and placement counselors at your college). Then you will creatively promote your benefits to make the largest number of people know of your availability in the shortest amount of time.

Your career search will be more fun and less lonely if you enlist the assistance of friends, relatives, coworkers, etc. to form a Brain Trust of advisors. Not only can they provide emotional support, but they can also serve as a valuable sounding board for ideas and for evaluating your efforts.

Keep written records of your activities.

Now you have the basic ingredients and the order in which they should be combined. You'll find writing down your own recipe helpful because you'll be able to recreate it in the future should you desire or be required to go through all this again.

Maintain a notebook to record all your plans, actions and results. You could refer to this notebook (road map) as your Career Journal. You don't always have to carry it with you. Just take notes during the day and copy them into your Journal later. Beginning your own personal Career Journal may be the single most important decision you make to achieve lasting career success.

Keeping your Career Journal up to date does not have to be a laborious process resulting in a document cast in stone, recording your every move. Instead, it should be viewed as the record of your evolving plan so you can periodically re-evaluate, fine-tune and if necessary later, duplicate it.

Job Search 101 is a self-implemented, action-oriented program. At the end of each chapter are assignments for you to complete before going on. These are designed so that as you perform each, you will create another segment of your plan.

Phase One Chapters.

The first six chapters will provide the information to create our plan. Chapter Seven will show you how to bring all this data together in the form of a specific, operational and measurable blueprint for your job-search activities.

Phase Two Chapters.

The next three chapters are devoted to performing on the interview itself. Chapter Eight presents the steps you need to take in order to prepare for and begin each interview. Chapter Nine brings you to the next step which is responding to the interviewer's questions and making a benefit-oriented presentation. Then Chapter Ten outlines ways to participate actively in the interview as you move into the final stage of asking for some commitment.

Phase Three Chapters.

The remainder of Job Search 101 demonstrates ways to evaluate your relative success vis-a-vis your specific objectives. You will learn to develop creative and professional ways to customize your job search to your needs and personality. And you will find out how to accept or decline an offer properly.

Job Search 101 is designed to stimulate your thinking for implementing your job search in a way that will make you stand out among your competitors in a positive way. In order for you to get the best perspective on your quest, and the variety of ways to address each phase of it, I suggest that you read Job Search 101 at least once before starting to implement the concepts that are presented. Use the book as a workbook, making notes in the margins as you read through it. Then, begin to implement each step and perform the assignments at the end of each chapter.

Every time you read Job Search 101 will be different from the last time. The creative stimulants in Chapter Twelve alone could provide you with many new ways to approach your search. Use this book as it was meant to be used: as a self-instructional, creative guide for making your period of unemployment as short and enjoyable as possible, concluding in a job that will be the most challenging, rewarding and profitable for you.

CHAPTER TWO

What Do You Have To Offer An Employer?

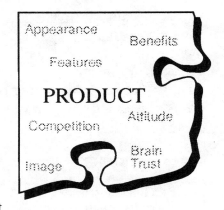

People generally buy products using a typical sequence of events. After the need is recognized, they seek information on the variety of products available in that category. They look at competitive products and compare the different attributes against a checklist they have established. The packaging affects the decision, as do the extra benefits the product offers, its price as compared to other "equal" products and the way in which it was promoted. Then the buyer makes a decision and purchases a product.

The employment-decision sequence.

Companies hire employees using virtually the same process. After the need is recognized, the company places an advertisement seeking candidates. The prospective employer narrows down the list of people to contact and interviews several to determine which one best meets the criteria the company has established. Many variables affect the evaluation, including the way the applicant appears, the level of income the candidate requires, any additional skills and experience that he offers and how professionally he presents himself. The decision is made and the job offered to the chosen individual.

Accordingly, the product that best meets the needs of the purchaser has the greatest likelihood of being chosen. Therefore, you must determine what you have to offer, and then investigate to whom these skills would provide the greatest benefit. Depending on your answers, you may have to make some changes in the product or search for different companies to which you can sell your existing product. No matter how hard you try, you won't be able to sell an apple to someone who wants to buy an orange. But if your prospect is looking for an apple, you have to demonstrate that yours is the best choice.

With this principle in mind, your first assignment is to perform some soul-searching into what you have to offer, what you want to do as far as a career is concerned, and how the answers to each relate to the other. You should be as objective and honest with yourself as possible.

Ask not what a company can do for you, but what you can do for the company.

You must think of these factors in terms that mean the most to the people who will purchase your product. Many applicants think in terms of features or the specific skills they have developed. On the other hand, most employers think in terms of the benefits the application of these skills will provide to the company. Therein lies the principle barrier to effective communication in an interview. You should understand the difference between these two perspectives and begin to think and talk in terms of benefits.

FEATURES, ADVANTAGES AND BENEFITS

A **feature** is a part of the product (experience, education, skills,etc); an **advantage** is the feature in action or <u>what it does</u>. And a **benefit** is a positive result of the action, or what the feature <u>does for the person</u> who is using the product. The differences are critical because you must realize that people don't actually buy a product as much as they buy what the product will do for them. An employer is not "buying" what you have done in the past as much as he is buying what you have to offer or what he thinks you can do for the company in the future. Here are examples of the way in which this concept should become integrated into your job search:

FEATURE	ADVANTAGE	BENEFIT
1. Graduated from college with 3.5 GPA.	Learned marketing skills.	Implemented marketing skills by increasing ads in college newspaper by 50%.
2. Promoted to manager.	Learned how to motivate people.	Increased profitability by 20% for each of last 2 years.
3. 5 years experience in finance.	Demonstrated skills in all aspects of personal financial planning.	Generated $X0,000 in new business by teaching seminars in personal financial planning.

EXAMPLE: The interviewer asks you what your grade point was in school. You answer using the above information about your benefits:

My total cumulative average was 3.5. But my GPA (Grade-Point Average) in my major, Marketing, was 4.0. I took this classroom information and demonstrated a real working knowledge of marketing while working at the school's newspaper. As the person responsible for selling advertising space, I used the techniques learned in class to increase ad revenue by 50% over my objective. I feel strongly that I could apply these same techniques for this company by…

Additionally, a benefit may be defined in three ways. It could be a **primary, secondary** or **"grabber"** benefit. A <u>primary</u> benefit is that which is most important to one particular interviewer at that particular time. For example, an interviewer for a department store may be impressed with the fact that you used to be an airline flight attendant. Your presentation should then revolve around the ways in which you could apply those skills to making customers more satisfied with their shopping experience at his store, thus generating increased business.

A <u>secondary</u> benefit is one that is less important at this particular time, but will add to your case for landing a job offer. In the interview just described, such a benefit could be the fact that you worked in your college's book store and gained experience in generating customer satisfaction that resulted in a 25% decrease in customer complaints. Note that this could be a primary benefit to a different interviewer.

And finally, a "grabber" is a benefit that is available for a limited time only. You may have a job offer pending and you must respond within two days, thus making you "available for a limited time only," pressuring the interviewer to make you an offer or lose you as a potential employee. Don't use this technique if you don't have an offer pending, because you could find yourself without any offer.

The best kept secret of a job search.

The concept of selling your benefits may be the most important idea in your career search. If you can uncover any particular interviewer's most important criteria for a candidate, you are much more likely to get an offer if you can demonstrate your ability to satisfy that need. You can find out what these needs are during your pre-interview research or by asking questions during the interview itself.

Your definition of your features, advantages and benefits can be broken down into two groups: quantifiable characteristics (education, years of experience, height, weight, etc.) and characteristics that you can qualify (attitude, quality of experience and education, etc.). It is imperative that you carefully review both.

Quantifiable Characteristics

You'll find it easier to begin by dealing with the aspects of your background that are easily measured. The courses you have taken, your grade-point average and the number of years of experience you have can be listed in concrete terms. Also consider your hobbies and general experiences (travel, family responsibilities, etc.) in your analysis.

1) THE TALENT-ANALYSIS SHEET.

It will be much easier to perform your research with the help of the Talent-Analysis Sheet, which will force you to think in terms of the accomplishments you achieved by implementing your features. The Talent-Analysis Sheet is a summary of every job and responsibility you have had, what you learned from each and what you accomplished with that knowledge. The information you compile by completing this form will "funnel" directly into your resume, making it easier to complete and more productive for you.

EXHIBIT 2: THE TALENT-ANALYSIS SHEET FOR YOUR EMPLOYMENT

1.Company Name: _____   Employment Dates: _____

Most Recent Job Title: _____

RESPONSIBILITY	SKILLS DEVELOPED	LIKED	DISLIKED	APPLICATION RESULTS

Below is an example of a completed Talent-Analysis Sheet. This person's most recent position with XYZ company was as Manager, Marketing Communications. One of the responsibilities in this position was to "Plan and Implement Advertising Strategy." One of the skills developed was "Budgeting." The person liked the creative opportunity this task provided, but disliked the lack of importance placed on the advertising function at this company. And the person saved the company $X,000 by applying this skill.

1. XYZ COMPANY   August 15, 1984 - Present

Manager, Marketing Communications; 1988 - Present

RESPONSIBILITY	SKILLS DEVELOPED	LIKED	DISLIKED	APPLICATION RESULTS
Plan and implement ad strategy	Budgeting	Creativity	Ad importance not appreciated by management	Saved $X,000 on the most recent ad by analyzing budgeted funds
Produce trade show exhibits to attract attention	Using graphics	Creativity	Detail work	Generated 50% more leads than last year
Produce Annual Report	Organization and communication skills	Meeting people in all corporate divisions	Coordinating details among all divisions and departments	Completed an award-winning annual report, acclaimed by shareholders

Trying to remember everything you have ever done could be overwhelming. Instead, chronologically list all the companies you have worked for, and write the name of each on a separate piece of paper as a header for that page. Below that, list the job title you held. Then divide the page into five columns with the headings as shown in Exhibit 2, which is the form you should use as a guide for doing this exercise.

Listing your features.

Write down every job responsibility you have ever performed, no matter how menial you think it may have been. Try to use words to describe them that will help you recall the activities you actually performed. Think of such activities as customer contact (answering the telephone or serving as a receptionist) and customer correspondence (typing letters) to add extra value to your performance.

Finding your advantages.

If you perform any function long enough, you should develop certain skills. Think about what you had to do to fulfill your responsibilities and list these in the column headed "SKILLS DEVELOPED." For example, when planning and implementing advertising strategy, you could develop skills in analytical problem solving, creative problem solving, budgeting, strategic media planning, organizing written presentations, teamwork, market research and analysis and making oral presentations.

Likes and dislikes.

Then list what you liked about implementing each skill. If you were in sales and listed a skill you developed as "Territory Planning," you should now think about how you performed this task. What did you like and dislike about doing it? Did you enjoy listing all your prospects and customers in order of their potential? Did you like analyzing the routing you would take each day to maximize your calls and minimize expenses and down time?

Or if you showed "Persuasion" as a skill, did you like closing the sale in person more than you liked doing it over the telephone? Are you good at making presentations in front of groups, or do you dread doing so? List all the aspects of each responsibility and skill that you liked and disliked, then add them to the appropriate column.

Accomplishments and benefits.

Finally, the column headed "APPLICATION RESULTS" requires you to list the specific accomplishments you achieved as a result of performing each particular skill to fulfill the responsibility you were assigned. The more specific you can be in terms of dollars saved, or the percentage increase in revenue that occurred as a result of your efforts, the more persuasive and effective your written and oral presentations will be.

Completing this form will force you to list as many responsibilities (features) that you can think of. It also compels you to think beyond the features, into the parts of the task that you liked and disliked and the skills you developed (advantages). These lead directly to the results of applying these skills (the benefits to the company). Write all this information in your Career Journal, and keep it up to date as you perform future activities.

Using the Talent-Analysis Sheet to review your education.

This form is easily adaptable to examining your education. As shown in Exhibit 3, list your major in place of the company name. Then place your specific subject where "Job Title" would otherwise be. Finally, fill out the remainder of the form according to the example shown below.

EXHIBIT 3: THE TALENT-ANALYSIS SHEET FOR YOUR EDUCATION

1. University of Cincinnati, Senior year

Marketing Courses

COURSE TITLE	SKILLS DEVELOPED	LIKED	DISLIKED	APPLICATION RESULTS
Sales Management	Planning and organizing	Learned how to motivate and lead people to be more productive	Possible need to to travel away from home every week	During a summer job selling at a retail store, I created a plan to better motivate the staff; reduced turnover by 10%
Advertising Strategy	Setting goals and creating plans to achieve them	Setting and achieving measurable objectives	Details of advertising research	Applied the principles of creative goal setting to my career plan; generated three job offers

As you continue your assessment of your education, list all the courses (features) you have taken, seminars attended, job training classes, etc. Then list the skills (advantages) you learned from these and, finally, the accomplishments you achieved (benefits) by implementing your knowledge.

Never discount the value of your experience in life itself. For example, I know of one time a mother with grown children sought a job. She had been out of the work force for more than fifteen years but was successful in presenting the benefits of what she had experienced in terms of time management, budgeting, discipline and "product" management.

Use the Talent-Analysis Sheet to list all the activities you have been associated with outside the formal arena and the benefits that resulted. Adapt it to review your likes and dislikes in your general activities and experience. Do you like assembling model cars? What about customizing real ones? What sports are you good at and which ones do you like most? What do you do in your leisure time? What do your friends like about you and what do they dislike? You can utilize your Brain Trust to help provide information.

The supreme courtship.

It's critical to have an ongoing relationship between education and experience in your life. Too many people think that education is one stage of life and experience is another. These, however, are neither mutually exclusive, nor do they end. Continuing your education and experience is both mutually supportive and necessary for continued career growth.

The fundamental "rules" for succeeding in any career will change over time. Heretofore "proven" theories become outdated, new technology replaces old, and the traditions of yesterday are replaced by the new practices of today. You must keep seeking current information and continue your education throughout your working life.

You can make an analogy between knowledge and a bucket of water with a hole in it. If you don't keep replacing the contents, it eventually trickles away. You must keep adding more to your bucket of skills in order to remain competitive in your job. Unless you're a recent graduate, a question you may hear during an interview is "What have you done to continue your education since graduation?" Your answer will provide a great deal of insight into your willingness to remain current.

2) PHYSICAL CONDITIONING.

There is one important responsibility that is often overlooked in a career search. Too frequently, people focus on conditioning their mind via continuing education and ignore the equally important necessity to condition their bodies. The health issues notwithstanding, good physical conditioning will add a great deal to your job search. A regular regimen of exercise provides the benefits of image, stamina and energy. The issue of stress reduction is equally applicable.

Related to good health is the image you portray. Your physical image is an important part of the package for your product, and it is one of the points that can add to or detract from your candidacy. Your physical image is enhanced by the clothes you wear, but it goes even further than that.

Finding the proper image for yourself does not necessitate plastic surgery. It means doing the best with what you have. Certain physical characteristics you cannot change. But others you can control, and you must exercise that control. If you need to lose or gain weight, do it. If you have facial hair, it will always have an impact on people, either positive or negative. If you feel you need to grow or remove facial hair, do it. Hair length and style will always make an impression, either positive or negative. Again, evaluate what you need to do with your hair and do it.

Don't make these changes simply to get the job, with the intention of going back to the "real you" later. It is a mistake to change your style just for the job and then revert to your old image after you begin working. In order to succeed in a job, you have to keep on doing the things you did to get it originally.

What is your energy policy?

Physical conditioning will also give you greater stamina to proceed with your job search. You'll have many late nights working on your correspondence, prospecting, etc, and a regular exercise regimen will help you deal with the stress resulting from worrying about the results of all your activities. A significant amount of stress can also be created by a day of continuous interviewing, followed by dinner with your "boss-to-be." You need to be as energetic at dinner as you were when you first arrived that morning. A healthy life style will help you through the day.

3) YOU ARE WHAT YOU WEAR.

Your physical image is enhanced by your clothes. Your choice of attire for your interview makes a clear statement about your personality and values. Clothes also make a difference in how you come across to others. You may have heard the expression that you never have a second chance to make a good first impression. Many people make value judgements about you based on your clothes and overall appearance. They size you up immediately and spend the remainder of the interview confirming their opinion.

You can make a good impression without having to go out and buy a new wardrobe. Read a book on dressing for success. Wear color-coordinated outfits, cleaned and pressed shirts and blouses. Shine your shoes and make sure your hands are clean. Take inventory of your wardrobe. A few extra dollars now for a new tie, blouse or pair of shoes can mean a great deal when you are on an interview. If you need to spend some money to bring your wardrobe up to date, do so. You'll find it to be a wise investment in your career success.

You can have the nicest clothes in the world, but Mother Nature can make them look terrible if you are caught in a wind, rain or snow storm. Your appearance on an interview is a function of the clothes you wear and how you look in them. If you arrive late, all disheveled with rain-soaked hair, you won't make a favorable impression. Make sure your inventory includes a briefcase-sized umbrella, a small can of hair spray and several combs.

4) COMPETITION.

As you are evaluating your product, you should do so in the context of the competition you will face in your field of interest. In slow economic times, the number of competitors will increase. Large layoffs and closing businesses indicate more people seeking work. You'll have to investigate the extent to which this affects your particular industry and job level.

These same conditions will affect the people with whom you will be competing. As those out of work seek income, they may be willing to take less pay and choose something below their present skill level, possibly placing them in your category or you in theirs. A careful reading of the want ads will offer an indication of the salary being offered, experience or education necessary and other criteria sought for individual positions. Just be aware that you may have someone with more experience competing with you for your position. In your presentation, you could anticipate this event, and turn it around so it becomes a positive point for you. You could say:

Although I may not have as much experience as others seeking this position, I feel that I am appropriately (or uniquely) qualified. If, during hard times, you hired someone who was over-qualified, that person would probably leave as soon as times got better. On the other hand, I will be sufficiently challenged and will therefore be more creative and industrious in the fulfillment of my responsibilities.

But if you are the person who is out of work, willing to take a lower-paying position in order to provide income, you have to approach the situation differently. The interviewer could confront you with the fact that you are over-qualified and may leave when times get better. You could answer in at least two different ways:

Mr. Smith, I don't anticipate that occurring, but it could be the situation at some point in time. Yet for whatever length of time I remain employed by you, my extensive experience will provide the company with greater results that will continue creating income for years after I leave. I would, in effect, be acting as a consultant.

Or, you could take a different approach, depending on your actual intentions:

Mr. Smith, perhaps I am overqualified for this particular position, but I am willing to take a cut in income now to secure a long-term opportunity. I would certainly feel indebted to a company that hired me in my time of need, and I would always work diligently and be a loyal employee in order to repay that company. Isn't that really the kind of employee you want working for you?

As you can see, there are a variety of ways to quantify your attributes. Use your Talent-Analysis Sheet to make a list of those regarding your education and experience. Add to that all the other conditions you feel warrant analysis such as your physical conditioning, clothes and competitive position. The resulting data will help you gain a better understanding of yourself and where your strengths and weaknesses lie. This task is easier for the quantifiable elements of your life than it is for those that you must qualify.

Characteristics You Can Qualify

Subjectivity can be applied at any point in your evaluation. Different people could have the same GPA, but be dissimilar in their application of their knowledge. Now that you know the fundamentals of your product, you have to begin to ask yourself "why" you liked and disliked various aspects of your experience and education.

1) THE POWER OF POSITIVE DOING.

In order to keep this perspective on your activities, it's important to have a positive and self-confident attitude. Such an attitude will allow you to be objectively and creatively critical of your history.

The way you sell yourself depends on how you see yourself. A positive attitude is a vital asset at any time in life, but it is of particular importance during a job-search period. A college graduate most likely has not experienced (and hopefully never will experience) the stress, self-doubt and ego damage that the loss of a job later in life can cause. But even that psychological damage will be less severe if the person has a healthy, relatively self-confident attitude.

Certain phrases can give you an indication of your attitude at any particular time. These are most likely to occur to you as you think during periods of mental relaxation. They can tell you how you are viewing your situation at that time, from a negative or positive frame of mind. If you dwell on negative thoughts, they can destroy your attitude and possibly success in your search. I call these <u>Career Killers</u>, and here are some examples:

CAREER KILLERS

What if I don't get a job?
What if I don't get this job?
How could I have been so stupid?
I don't meet all their requirements, so why bother applying?
I don't have a college (or high school, or graduate) degree, so they'll never hire me.
People aren't available on Monday mornings or Friday afternoons, so I'll call later.
That job is beyond my skill level.
I don't need to prepare for this interview. I'll just "wing" it.
I'm too young, old, inexperienced, etc.
I'm not worth that much money, so why bother asking for it?
That won't work, so I won't waste my time doing it.
I can't ...
They won't ...
I'll never .....
It's useless to ...
Why me?
I'm not a ...
I wish I could ...
Yes, but ...
What would my (parents, spouse, significant other) want me to do?
What would my (parents, spouse, significant other) say if I...?
If I was only more ...
If only I had ...
If this idea could work, somebody would have already tried it.
What if I get on the job and find out I can't do it?
What will people think of me if I fail?

Just say Yes!

Dwell instead on all the positive benefits you have to offer. Think about what you can do, not what you can't. If any of the above thoughts come into your mind, it's very important that you recognize the negative effects they can have. Think "I can..." or "I will ..." and you will be much more successful in your search and later on the job. Use the self-affirming expressions listed below to keep your mental train of thought on the right track.

SELF-AFFIRMING EXPRESSIONS

I know I can ... if only given the chance.
As soon as I start work, I'll ...
I will ...
It's always helpful to ...
Why not try ...
I can ...
This is great and I'm for it 100%.
I feel good about ...
I did a good job at ...
I am a good (positive noun).
I can make this work by ...
If it's to be, it's up to me.
I know I'm good at ...
I'm worth that much money because ...
If they didn't think I could do the job, they wouldn't have hired me.
In how many other ways can I ...
What if I tried (some positive action)?
I feel good about myself because ...
I'm the best there is at ...

Control your ego.

As you can see, you should maintain a self-confident attitude, though you shouldn't let it get out of control to the point that you come across as an egotist. It's been said that conceit is a condition that makes everyone sick but the person who has it.

Your attitude about yourself is clearly evident in your words and actions. It's good to state your accomplishments accurately, but leave out the superlatives. Let your results speak for themselves. Let others testify to your superior abilities through your use of testimonials and references. Use the word "we" instead of "I" wherever you worked with others to achieve a goal. Rarely is one person totally responsible for the superior results of an organization or action.

"We Three Kings..."

There are at least three "givens" that you should be aware of before you start your job search. Among them is the fact just mentioned, that you will be rejected most of the time, and you can't let this destroy your self-confidence. Second, the prospective employer is never in as much of a hurry as you are to make a decision. And finally, you can't give up. You must always remember that "If it's to be, it's up to me."

Number one: Dealing with a 99.8% rejection rate.

By its very nature, your career pursuit will generate many negative responses. You'll apply to many more jobs than you'll receive offers for. There is an excellent graphic depiction of the interviewing process made by a writer who filled a page with the word "No," except in the very bottom right corner of the page where was found the word "Yes." The ratio of "No" to "Yes" answers is enormously large. If you know that from the start, it may not be as destructive to your self-confidence.

During an average job search, you could easily mail more than 500 unsolicited letters, from which you may receive about 100 responses. Ninety six of these will be of the "thanks-but-no-thanks" variety. Four will request a resume for further consideration. Two could result in interviews, and one of those should produce an offer. 80% of the people will ignore you. You'll be rejected by 99.8% of the 20% that respond, which means that generally only .2% of your total contacts will offer you a position.

Yet through it all, you must maintain the optimistic feeling that if you keep at it, something positive has to happen. Remind yourself that the prospective employer is not rejecting you personally: she is rejecting the fit between the skills you offered and those required for that specific position. You are still a marketable product, but not for that particular company.

Loss of self-confidence can also extend the time of your search, since a poor self-image is obvious during an interview. An interviewer can immediately tell the way candidates feel about themselves by the way they carry themselves. Self-image is evident in their posture, tone and volume of voice, and eye communication, among other things. Given the choice between equally qualified candidates, an interviewer will probably offer the position to the more confident of two competitors, leaving the other to continue in search of a position.

Number two: People make decisions too slowly.

Not all employers move as quickly as you would like to have them move. You'll hear many excuses for delaying the interviewing process. For example, I've been told by professional "head hunters" (employment agents) that in January and February people don't interview because they are either in the start-of-the-year blues or they are just getting back from the holidays and haven't gotten "in the groove" yet. In April and May, employers are getting Spring fever, sales are going well and they just don't have time to talk with candidates now, or they are preparing for summer vacations. Of course, from June through August they are on vacation and can't talk with you. September and October always bring budget tightening, so new positions are being placed on hold and existing openings will be filled after the first of the year when the new budget takes effect. And as we all know, companies just don't hire people during the Christmas Holiday period.

According to these "professionals," March is the only month in which there isn't a delay in the interviewing process. I'm sure they don't believe that nonsense, and they are just trying to make people feel good because there is no activity in their job search. But you can't afford to listen to them. You have to implement the strategies and tactics described in Job Search 101, take the bull by the horns and go out and get a job.

Of course people go on vacation during the summer months. But not everybody in the company does. And there are always numerous people with whom you will have to interview, so you can start with those who are still in the office. Or use down-time to do your prospecting and qualifying work, re-think your resume and cover letter, make telephone calls to learn more about your target company's product line and search for actions to take that will bring you closer to your goals.

Rules of thumb.

There are two rules of thumb regarding the length of time it takes to find a job. One is that you should expect to take at least one month to find a job for each $ 10,000 of income you want. The other is that you should expect to take about a week for each $ 1,000 of expected income. Given a choice, you'd probably take the former formula. But when you are out of work, you don't have the luxury of waiting. You have to find something in the shortest time frame possible. The techniques described in Job Search 101 will help you shorten that period. You just need to be aware that it will take some time, and you can't let that fact get you down.

Number three: You can't give up.

You have to keep at your search no matter who's on vacation, no matter what the newspapers say about the economy and no matter how many rejection letters you receive. You have to look at those rejection letters with a positive outlook. If you were doing nothing to get a job, you wouldn't get any such letters. Therefore, the very fact that you are getting them means that you are headed in the right direction. You have to think that everything happens for a reason but the reason may not be evident until after it happens.

Keep your focus on what is good and right for you. Attend support-group meetings, talk with friends and relatives, keep a file of reference letters you have received and regularly read them, read self-help books, listen to motivational tapes, and by all means read and follow the instructions given in Job Search 101. Maintain your self-confident attitude in the face of all the negative responses that are sure to come your way.

Think in terms of what can go right or what you can do to improve the situation. Challenge yourself to redirect your thinking to the positive possibilities. Change "What will I do if I don't get this job?" to "When they do offer me this job, how can I make them believe they made the right choice? How could I do more than they expect?"

Burn some bridges.

You may have heard the expression "Don't burn your bridges." This adage is true when referring to other people. But if you look at it in a different context, it becomes valid to burn some bridges to eliminate a means of retreat. You have to rid yourself of excuses that you use to explain or excuse your relative lack of success in your job search. If you hear yourself saying you're "too (young, old, inexperienced, qualified, poor, rich, etc)," you could be allowing yourself a mental means of retreat when you become discouraged. You have to eliminate those thoughts from your mental vocabulary.

Making up excuses is the easy way out. It takes more creativity and work to overcome your excuses than it does to allow them to overcome you. Generally speaking, it won't be the particular "flaw" or situation that will prevent you from getting a job. It's you're attitude toward it that will more than likely be the culprit. Exorcise your excuses. Figuratively burn any bridges that will allow you a mental means of retreat, and you'll find yourself creating methods to succeed where you never thought they existed.

2) THE SELF-ANALYSIS BALANCE SHEET.

Just as the Talent-Analysis Sheet organized your thinking around your quantifiable attributes, the Self-Assessment Balance Sheet as shown in Exhibit 4 will help you organize and analyze your strengths and weaknesses. It is set up as an accounting ledger, so you can list your Strengths (Assets) in the left-hand column, and your Weaknesses (Liabilities) in the right. You could begin by placing all the activities you liked, as listed on your Talent-Analysis Sheet, in the "Strengths" column. Then take all the activities you disliked and place them in the "Weaknesses" column.

EXHIBIT 4: THE SELF-ANALYSIS BALANCE SHEET

STRENGTHS	WEAKNESSES
Creative	Oral Communications
Optimistic	Self-confidence
Marketing Professional	Overweight
Determined	Procrastination
Sales-Training Experience	Detail Work
Hardworking	Follow Through
Problem Solving	Stubborn
Marketing Communications	
Planning Skills	
Strong Writing Skills	
Personable	
MBA	
Self-Motivated	
Energetic and Competitive	
Healthy	
Family, Friends	
Mature	
Good Listener	
Goal Oriented	

Use the Self-Analysis Balance Sheet to target weak areas for increased attention. You will readily see traits that are not as strong as you would like them to be and you can then develop ways to strengthen them.

The Self-Analysis Balance Sheet will also serve you well during an interview. Invariably you will be asked to discuss your strengths and weaknesses. As you think back to this Balance Sheet, you will be able to recite your strengths. But more importantly, you'll be able to demonstrate your insight into your weaknesses and show that you have a plan in place to improve them.

You may find it helpful to seek an "outside opinion" to help give you more objectivity. Consult your spouse, significant other, friends, former employers, relatives, etc. for a frank analysis of your weak areas. An "exit interview" is a particularly good source for input into this form. During such an interview, people are more likely to be candid and objective since they have nothing to lose by so doing.

Interview yourself.

A different perspective may also provide input into this chart. Take some quiet time and just ask yourself questions. Use the list of questions interviewers are likely to ask you (a list of these can be found in Exhibit 25) and honestly answer them to yourself. What makes you feel good about yourself? What does your "gut" tell you?

What do you want to be when you grow up?

Determining the actual career in which you can apply your skills can be the most important decision you make. There is no formula for helping you decide it, and all you can really do is to follow your instincts. You can find directories in the library that will list potential vocations, but these don't go into great lengths to describe the functions and opportunities you will be expected to perform.

Hopefully, the forms you completed in Exhibits 2 and 4 will provide you with insight into the type of work you like most and the areas in which you have the strongest assets. As you go on informational interviews (as described in Chapter Eight), you could ask questions of the people to find out how your skills might be applied in their particular field.

There is always professional help upon which you can rely. Career counselors can give you tests to help you direct your thinking toward one career or another. These can be aptitude tests or vocation test, and they can provide input into your decision.

The Tombstone Test.

There is one technique that could help define what you want to do with your life. It's called the Tombstone Test. You simply write what you want to appear on your tombstone (i.e., how you want to be remembered), and it should provide direction for you.

Once Upon a Time...

One question that you should always keep in mind, especially when you find yourself mentally getting down, is "What is good about my situation right now?" This question will force you to take a serious look at your present environment and provide you with ideas on how to make it better. Perhaps a short case history will illustrate this thought.

I was told one evening at about 5:00 pm that my services for my company were no longer required. There was no two-week notice or severance pay. I was in my hotel room when the conversation was held, so I could have stayed there and left the next morning to make the four-hour drive home. I chose to leave immediately so I could have the entire following day (Friday) to begin my new career search.

During the drive home, I thought about the benefits of my present situation and the positive aspects of my life that could be useful in this new search. I took out a sheet of paper and along the left edge wrote the numbers 1 through 20. I couldn't even think of one positive thing at the time. But I knew there had to be something good about my present situation, and I was determined to come up with 20 examples. Here is the list which I compiled during the drive home:

1. Family support.

2. Experience in getting a job.

3. Self-confidence.

4. The chance to start my own business (something I had always wanted to do).

5. I had a directory of all the companies in my field of interest that I could use as an immediate prospect list.

6. I had suspected this decision was forthcoming, and I already had some leads in place.

7. I had a good reputation in the business, and I knew I could get good references.

8. Friends whom I knew would offer support.

9. My computer was in good working order since I had just had it serviced.

10. My printer already had mechanicals for my personal letterhead at his print shop, and this could be re-ordered immediately.

11. Knowledge that I could always get "a job," perhaps not one that would pay as well, but one that would support me until I could get something better (not a good approach to a job search, but at the time it offered me consolation).

12. Enough money in the bank to last two months.

13. Good health.

14. Faith in my ability and attitude.

15. My brother had offered financial support to help get my twin sons through college if this expected unemployment situation eventually happened.

16. Fifteen years of experience in my chosen industry.

17. A car that worked properly and was in no need of major repair work.

18. No major personal expenses (other than college) that would come due in the near future.

19. My wife was working, and her insurance covered the entire family.

20. I had a library of self-help books and tapes that I could read and listen to.

There may be some duplication of thought in this list, but I hope you see that the thinking behind it was as important as the list itself. I always keep the original on file so I can look back on it periodically for a reminder that there is always something good in a situation if you look hard enough for it. And because I focused on what was good about my present situation, I even stopped on the way home to make several telephone calls to take some positive action.

Consider all aspects of your life. How is your credit? What will you need to do to keep it good (creditors are generally more willing to work with you during times of fiscal crisis if you keep them informed). If necessary, could you live with another family member until the crisis is over? Is it time to make a career change or perhaps go back to school and get your undergraduate or graduate degree?

What about the option of joining the military? If your long-term goal is to become a pilot, for example, the military could provide an excellent way for you to build up your hours in the air. Other training is available for a wide variety of vocations. Just take time to evaluate carefully and honestly what you need to do to improve your situation and what strengths you have available to use as your foundation for future success.

A little help from your friends.

Numbers 1, 7, 8, 10, 15 and 19 in the list above point out areas in which the support of other people is necessary. You must seek the assistance of other people in your career search. Think about whom you can call to implement your networking strategy. Use your Brain Trust to its fullest extent.

I was lucky to have such a group during each of my searches. The nucleus always remained the same, but other "board" members were added or deleted, depending upon my situation at the time. I can't stress enough the emotional support you'll get from knowing that you are not going through your job search alone. If you look around, you'll find people rooting for you, willing to help, and ready to offer that much-needed positive feedback and support. Don't overlook this vital asset.

I would like to end this chapter with the credo I repeat to myself every morning and try to live by each day. In fact, I have done this every day for over fifteen years. I didn't write this, but I have modified it slightly. I found it in the book <u>Live and Be Free Thru PSYCHO-CYBERNET-ICS</u> (Maxwell Maltz, M.D., F.I.C.S., and Charles Schreiber, F.A.R.A.; Warner Books Edition; First Printing: June, 1976). I recommend that you adapt it to your need, and say it to yourself regularly. My version has helped me get through many trying times, and perhaps yours will do the same for you.

This is the beginning of a new day. I have been given this day to use as I will. What I do today is important because I am exchanging a new day of my life for it. When tomorrow comes, this day will be gone forever, leaving in its place whatever I have traded for it. I pledge to myself that it shall be for good, gain and success in order that I shall not regret the price I paid for this day.

My thinking and my attitudes are calm and cheerful. I act and feel friendly toward other people. I am tolerant of other people, their shortcomings and mistakes, and I view their actions with the most favorable understanding possible.

I act as though attainment of my goals is sure to happen. I am the kind of individual I aspire to be, and everything I do and the way I feel expresses this individuality.

I will not allow my judgment or my attitudes to be affected by negativism or pessimism. I will smile as often as possible, at least several times a day.

I will respond in a calm and intelligent manner, without alarm, no matter what the situation. If I cannot control the situation, I will respond in a positive manner, even to negative facts.

ASSIGNMENTS:

2.1 Create a Talent-Analysis Sheet for your employment and education.

2.2 Create a Self-Analysis Balance Sheet. List all the strengths you can think of; then list all your weaknesses.

2.3 List the activities you can perform to strengthen these areas.

2.4 Write a one-sentence summary of your major benefits and aspirations and why you feel a company can benefit by hiring you. Think of this as a classified ad you are writing about yourself.

2.5 Create your "Brain Trust" of associates, family and friends. Talk to them and explain your situation and objective.

2.6 Write down the date by which you must have a new position.

2.7 Make a list of twenty things that are good about your situation right now.

2.8 Set aside time to think about all the information you have gathered and try to determine exactly what it is you want to do for your career's work.

2.9 What excuses do you have that you use to explain your lack of success in your job search? What are five ways you can turn these around into a reasons for hiring you?

CHAPTER THREE

How To Be In The Right Place At The Right Time

In a marketing sense, place decisions have two different applications. First you must consider the physical location in which you will market your product, including an evaluation of the positive and negative factors associated with doing business in different countries, regions, states and even cities. In a career sense, you must similarly compare the geographic areas that offer the greatest opportunities for success in your job search. After weighing all the relevant criteria, you then make a decision about your career location.

Second, you must decide what methods of distribution you will use to get your product to the end user. Career-wise, you may choose to go directly to the prospective employer by sending your resume in response to an ad. On the other hand, you may choose to utilize the services of one or more of the professional people whose job it is to find you an employment opportunity. Or you may choose a combination of both.

Physical Location

In retailing, the three most important decision criteria for choosing the place to establish a business are 1) location, 2) location and 3) location. These same decision criteria are required for career success.

You can have the most outstanding skills and benefits to offer an employer, but nobody will buy them if the positions lie elsewhere. If you want to maximize your career opportunities and income, you have to find out where the market offers the greatest chances for success. While you may hope the location will be where you presently live, your career may require a move to another city or part of the country.

International opportunities.

In a broad sense, you should consider the continent on which you will seek employment. Many international career opportunities are available on other continents or perhaps as close as Mexico or Canada. With the world as your market, your chances of finding employment are greatly increased.

Following the Persian-Gulf war, many opportunities appeared for Western companies. These ran the gamut, from people needed to help rebuild the oil fields ravaged during the war, to public relations and other service firms required to assist in the economic reconstruction. While these may be considered temporary assignments, an enormous amount of experience and education may be garnered from such a tour of duty.

Domestic opportunities.

If you decide that you want to work in the United States, give careful thought to the benefits of the region that presents the best opportunity for your chosen field. If you are in the commercial aviation industry, the Northwest offers opportunities. The oil fields of Texas and Oklahoma provide careers for interested people. The entertainment business is centered in Southern California, and the advertising field is headquartered in New York City. Certainly jobs are available in these industries in cities all around the country. But if you want to "make it big," you'll probably end up where the greatest concentration of jobs is located. Obviously, your competition will be greater where the leaders are established.

When deciding where to live, establish criteria that are important to you. For instance, if you don't deal with heat well, you probably wouldn't like to live in the Southeast or Southwest. Also, think of the cost-of-living differences among regions. Buy newspapers to find out about a city, its life style, sporting events, employment opportunities, housing costs or the arts. Gather as much data as you can about whatever interests or concerns you and the significant others in your life who influence, and will be influenced by, your ultimate decision.

It's very easy to get information about distant cities. Simply contact a local realtor or the local chamber of commerce, and you will be inundated with details on many topics. If you've recently had a class reunion, look in the "directory" to find out what classmates are in the city of your choice, and call them. Perhaps a nearby store sells out-of-town newspapers, or you could subscribe to your target city's newspaper.

If you choose to have a professional moving company relocate you, you could look into United Van Lines. They have a service called "Molly Malone" that provides a great deal of information about your destination city. For details on this, you can call Bay State Moving Systems, a United Van Lines agent, at 1-800-628-9360.

Whatever your location criteria are, write them down in order of priority and use them to evaluate your decision. You can adapt the Self-Analysis Balance Sheet to this task. Under the "Strengths" column, list all the benefits of a particular area. Under the "Weaknesses" column, list all the negative factors. Then weigh these against your list of criteria.

There are ways to stay in one region and still work for a company based in another part of the country or the world, for that matter. If you are in sales, for example, you could work in a local territory for a national company. But you may just be delaying the inevitable. If you ever want to move up in that organization, it will invariably require a move to another location. By making the decision to move close to the home office early in your career, the long-term negative effects could be reduced.

Now that you have chosen the opportune physical location, you have to determine what resources are available to assist you and whether or not you want to utilize their services.

Product Distribution

Exhibit 5 charts the variety of courses available to you. As it shows, you have two basic ways to "distribute" your product. You can go directly to the prospective employer, or you can use the services of middlemen to assist you. Their assistance can be valuable, but there is also a fee for it. However, when all factors are considered, it will behoove you to use every tool at your disposal, and that includes some combination of these channels.

Many people and companies are available to assist in your quest for employment. The major benefit they all offer is the ability to magnify your job-search efforts by helping you find additional people to contact or by finding them for you. They can also serve as another resource for input and feedback on your correspondence and interviewing skills.

EXHIBIT 5: CHANNELS OF DISTRIBUTION

DIRECT   **THROUGH MIDDLEMEN**

```
DIRECT                         THROUGH MIDDLEMEN

  You                                    You

Newspaper        Employment                  State
  Ads             Agents                   Agencies

                           Career                    College
Networking              Consultants                   Staff

                  Temporary
 Direct          Assignment
  Mail

Prospective               Prospective Employer
 Employer
```

1) GOING DIRECTLY TO THE EMPLOYER.

Examples of going directly to a decision maker would be making a cold call or responding to an ad. The promotion tactics described in Chapter Five are all devoted to helping you market yourself in this fashion.

A benefit of this technique is that there is no fee involved, and given a choice among equal candidates, the company may choose the one that doesn't cost them any money. Another benefit of direct contact is that nobody knows as much about your product as you do or can sell your benefits as well as you can.

On the negative side you'll send out resumes and go on interviews that are not right for you because you didn't screen the opportunities as carefully as you could have. If you don't narrow down your job prospects to those that are related to your interests and goals, you could waste valuable time making contacts with people who you'll later find have no need for or interest in your services, or you in theirs.

Professional "Temping."

There are temporary positions available that could augment your income while you are searching for a permanent position. They may be secretarial positions for a few hours a day or "free-lance" executive positions. The field of professional temping is growing rapidly. Management, healthcare and even media service opportunities are available on a full-time yet temporary basis.

If you wanted to go directly to the prospective employer for a professional temporary position, you could use a letter similar to that shown in Exhibit 6, which you would send to companies advertising in the newspaper for a full-time employee. For example, find a company advertising to fill a position in your specialty. Send them this letter and follow it up with a telephone call.

EXHIBIT 6: EXAMPLE OF A LETTER SEEKING A TEMPORARY POSITION

Dear Name:

Your ad in Sunday's newspaper sought a (title). I feel that I could make a major contribution to (company name) in that position, but on a temporary basis. There are many advantages to (company name) for hiring me as your **temporary** (title):

- You will have the benefit of my <u>sixteen years of sales, marketing and management experience</u>. I have demonstrated superior achievement in the creation and implementation of successful sales and marketing strategy.

- I can serve as an <u>outside viewpoint</u> to stimulate innovative thinking among those "too close to the forest."

- <u>You'll save at least one-third</u> of the expense of hiring a full-time person, since you won't have to pay me for any benefits, holidays, vacations or days off due to illness.

- <u>You will minimize your risk</u> of making a bad hiring decision. If you don't think you are getting your money's worth, you can simply end the relationship without complications.

- <u>You can maximize the return on your investment</u>. Since I will work only when you feel the conditions require my expertise, there is no cost to you for any "down time."

- <u>You'll customize your personnel expenditures</u>. You can employ me on a daily, weekly or monthly fee schedule, whichever works out best for your needs. You pay only for the time I am on the job and productive.

If this proposal sounds as if it warrants further discussion under your particular circumstances, please give me a call at (312) 555-1234 so that we may discuss the concept in more detail. Thank you.

There are many benefits to you for taking this route. It provides a temporary source of income, and you can usually command a higher rate than normal because the client is saving 33% or more by not paying your benefits. At the same time, you are gathering valuable experience and making contacts that could lead to full-time employment later. And you can generally work around your own schedule, leaving time for other job-search activities.

A resource for more information on this topic is the book called <u>Professional Temping, A Guide to Bridging Career Gaps</u>. It was written by Eve Broudy and published by Collier Books, Macmillan Publishing Company, 866 Third Avenue, New York, New York, 10022.

2) DISTRIBUTION THROUGH MIDDLEMEN.

Employment agencies.

To support your efforts, you could use middlemen such as employment agencies. Some specialize in one field, for example in the automotive or healthcare industries. Others specialize in a specific function, cutting across industry boundaries. They could assist you in locating a position in marketing, sales, computer processing or accounting, among others. These people, for a fee, will take your credentials to the end user and begin the sales process for you. Their services are most applicable in Phase One of your job search, and you'll still have to go on the interviews and sell yourself to the prospective employer.

There are benefits to using employment agents. They may know of opportunities that are available but are not currently in the papers. They can also give you background on the position to help prepare you for the interview. And they can screen openings for you so you don't waste your time pursuing dead ends.

On the down side, they will try to market the most saleable and current product. If you have been registered with an agency for any length of time, you become less of a "hot" product, and they may lose interest in you. Keep contacting them on a regular basis to keep them aware of your benefits and interests. Similarly, let them know when you have secured other employment so they can direct their attention to their other clients.

You can locate employment agencies in the Yellow Pages or through advertising in the newspapers. Look for those that specialize in your field. Some specialize in a certain age bracket, such as 40 Plus. Then evaluate their services and fees, and always get a copy of their agreement and read the fine print. Under some conditions, you may be liable for the entire cost even if it is a "Fee Paid" position.

Temporary assignments.

Some agencies deal only with locating temporary assignments for secretarial positions. These may offer a way for you to augment your income while you are searching for full-time employment. They also provide an excellent way to gain additional experience, testimonials, references, etc.

Others specialize in finding positions for professional "temps." If you choose not to solicit such a job directly, you could contact an agency that will do it for you. One such agency is Management Assistance Group, 10 North Main Street, West Hartford, CT 06107. The president of this firm is Mr. John Tracey, Jr., and his telephone number is (203) 523-0000. Another is Savants, Inc., 12 Norcross Street, Suite 200, Roswell, GA, 30075. You can contact Scott Maxwell there at (404) 587-3234. A more complete listing can be found in Eve Broudy's book.

Career consultants.

You can also choose personal consultants for assistance in your career search. These are people who do not actually find you a position. They show you ways in which you can improve your ability to get a job. Among other things, they show you how to write a resume and successful letters, how to interview, how to groom yourself, and they should give you other important advice that could help you obtain employment. You in effect chose this avenue when you purchased Job Search 101.

Depending on the consultants you choose, they may be qualified to administer and interpret career tests. These are designed to help you decide upon a career, or they could be personality tests to help you get a better understanding of the "real" you.

State agencies.

State employment agencies offer a wide variety of services, at no charge to you. Primarily, they act as an employment agency. The positions they have available are not for just unskilled people, although they do have openings for them. They have a wide variety of opportunities in many different industries and specialties. These are posted or on microfilm for general viewing. Or you may go in and register to see an agent who will offer counseling and other assistance.

College placement services.

Depending on the college you are attending or have attended, its Career Development Office may offer many valuable services. For example, they can alert you to companies coming on campus to interview students and provide valuable background information on the companies themselves. Most provide resume-writing assistance and suggestions for improving your cover letter and interviewing skills. Others offer "mock" interviews for the students to practice their interviewing skills. Many provide lifetime assistance for their alumni, too.

3) THE GREAT DILEMMA.

Your next question probably is "Which do I use, the direct or indirect method?" In order to maximize your search efforts, you should use a combination of these. If you don't have a great deal of time for your search, you will probably go directly to the decision maker and through employment agencies to help you find a position. On the other hand, if you have more time, career counselors could be a valuable adjunct to your search, particularly if you need assistance in determining your eventual career.

Carefully consider using every resource at your disposal to assist in your endeavors. Use them to serve as members of your Brain Trust to provide you with useful and objective feedback. They are another weapon in your arsenal to utilize as you see fit, in a way that will provide the most long-term benefit for you.

ASSIGNMENTS:

3.1 Make a list of all the decision criteria you will use for evaluating the geographic areas that present the greatest employment opportunities in your specialty. Rank them in order of importance.

3.2 Begin to evaluate location options against this list until you decide where you want to seek employment.

3.3 Seek information on middlemen and contact those that meet your needs. Decide which, if any, you will utilize.

CHAPTER FOUR

How To Determine Your Market Price

The decision about how much you will charge for your services is one of the most important decisions you will make. In the world of marketing, prices are determined in a variety of ways, but the method used should always be based on achieving overall marketing objectives, with a variety of factors in mind.

In a career sense, you have to consider these same factors when making your pricing decisions. But the final decision always comes back to the objectives you have set for yourself. Some examples of career-pricing objectives are the following:

1. Return on your investment in your education.
2. Maximum long-term disposable income.
3. Maximum short-term disposable income.
4. Immediate purchase.
5. Long-term growth.
6. Enhance the perceived value of your benefits.
7. Cover your total costs.

How to achieve these objectives strategically.

Once you have determined your overall pricing objectives, there are three general strategies to consider:

1) A "skimming" strategy.

By implementing this strategic pricing approach, you offer your services at a price that is <u>higher</u> than the typical market price in your industry or geographic location. You will be limiting your opportunities, and probably extending the time of your search, but you will be addressing your objectives with longer-term implications. This strategy is not recommended if you are looking for an "immediate purchase" of your services.

If you have well-developed skills in a particular field that is less competitive, a skimming strategy could be successfully utilized. Or if you are seeking a temporary professional position, you may justifiably want to price yourself above what a full-time employee would make because the employer is not paying your benefits.

2) Market-Penetration pricing.

If your objectives have a shorter-term orientation, you could chose a "penetration" strategy. In so doing, you would <u>set your price low</u> enough to cover your costs and at a level that is below the general market price for someone with your skills and education. The general economic conditions may require that you pursue this strategy, especially if your competitors are selling their services at a lower price.

3) Combination.

The third strategy is a combination of the other two and provides you with the flexibility to respond to various situations. You don't have to set one price for your services and steadfastly adhere to it. As you perform pre-interview research into a company, investigate opportunities to adjust your salary request either up or down. Remember that your total income package is made up of wage and non-wage compensation. You may be able to balance a lower salary with a higher commission structure, stock options, a 401K plan, etc. And the mix of these factors could change for each job opportunity.

Gross vs. net income.

Maintain your focus on your net income. A gross income of $40,000, for example, could yield several different "take-home" amounts, depending on the extent to which the company pays the premiums for your insurance. Your disposable income could change dramatically given the variety of total compensation combinations available to you. It can also vary depending on the nature and amount of deductions from your pay.

In order for you to set the strategy that will achieve your overall price objectives, you must be aware of the numerous factors that will influence your decision. Some are external factors, beyond your control. Others are internal, under your control.

External Factors

1) Market conditions.

Given the state of the economy in your particular region and industry, your pricing options may be limited. In times of recession, the number of people seeking employment will increase. As supply begins to exceed demand, you may have to adjust your income expectations in order to remain competitive. You can command a higher price in the good times when there is economic growth and less competition for jobs. But in slower times, you may have to tighten your belt and seek a lower market price.

2) The employer's preconceptions.

Some prospective employers will view your price as an indicator of relative product quality. A candidate with a Master's Degree who prices him or herself below the level considered reasonable for that degree may not be viewed to offer as much value as one with a higher price. On the other hand, a price that the employer thinks is too high could label you as unreasonable or egotistical.

Similarly, some companies want to hire only those from prestigious schools and will be willing to pay more to get their graduates. Other companies have certain "personalities" that they want to hire and may be more willing to pay more for people with those personalities. This information should come out in your pre-interview research.

3) Wage standards.

Many companies have pay grades, and they may be unwilling or unable to deviate from these scales. If they have a given salary for a particular job title, they will not offer more. To do so would upset the structure of the salaries of all their other employees, and most companies are unwilling to do that. The existence of pay grades opens the door for negotiating non-wage incentives and benefits.

Internal Factors

1) Costs.

Your price should cover your costs, plus allow for a fair profit. The formula at the end of this chapter shows how the profit issue is taken into account. But if your costs are significant, you may have to take less profit in order to keep your price competitive. If your expenses are too high, you should take a serious look at lowering them.

2) Distinctiveness.

If you can demonstrate that you offer more benefits than your competitors do, you will be able to implement a skimming strategy. Charging a higher price can be done by effectively promoting and presenting your qualifications. The use of such a strategy points out the critical need to talk about the benefits you can offer a company, rather than simply stating your features. If the prospective employer feels that the company will be better off hiring you than one of your competitors, they will do so. It's up to you to convince them of your additional value.

3) Geographic location.

The region in which you choose to live will have a bearing on your pricing strategy. It must be used as input into your price decision because it obviously costs more to live in certain parts of the country than others. Read national newspapers to get a flavor for areas of opportunity. For example, the <u>National Employment Business Weekly</u> periodically provides information about the salaries being offered for your position and the relative costs of living for cities around the country. You need to get accurate information about salaries and costs of living to include in the pricing formula.

4) Education.

You should also consider the investment you have made in your education. Depending on the market needs, you could implement a penetration pricing strategy with a high-school or college degree and perhaps a skimming strategy with a graduate degree. Go back to your Talent-Analysis Sheet and take into account all the honors and awards you have received. What courses did you take that are particularly applicable to a specific employer? How have you continued your education since leaving college? How have you used your education to create more benefits for a prospective employer than your competitors have?

5) Psychic income.

There are benefits you may substitute for monetary income. You may choose perquisites ("perks") in lieu of a higher salary. Club memberships, job security, a big title or a corner office are examples of items that can make up a portion of your total "income." Carefully consider the impact on your net income of each different combination of wage and non-wage compensation.

6) Unique benefits.

Consider what special skills you bring to the market. An ex-athlete who was famous at the home-town college may have a price advantage there. Are you a Phi Beta Kappa? An accomplished musician? What extraordinary achievements have you made that will add value to your candidacy? How can you translate them into greater benefits for your employer?

7) Employment agent's fees.

If you choose to use an employment agent to help you find a job, he will charge a fee for his services. Generally the employer pays this fee, and it could amount to 30% of your starting salary. The hiring company may consider this amount when they make you an offer. They won't deduct the entire amount from the offer, but the bottom line could take the fee into consideration. The agent's fee is obviously an item that you cannot control, but you do have control over the decision to use his services or not.

How to get paid what you are worth.

Every job-interviewing situation will eventually get around to the question "What are your salary requirements?" The question generally won't be asked on the first interview, but it will more likely be asked on the second. You can approach the subject in two ways. First, you could give the salary range in which you would consider an offer. Second, you could have a specific figure in mind, which would be firm or negotiable, depending on your strategy.

1) Give the interviewer a salary range.

If you are open to negotiating a final compensation package, you may offer an upper and lower salary figure. You could give this range as "between $30,000 and $35,000" or you could say something to the effect of "in the low $30,000 area" or even "around $32,000 to $35,000." This technique will keep you in the running if your range is a little above what they wanted to pay. It demonstrates that you are trying to be reasonable and that you are also willing to negotiate. And by indicating you are willing to bargain, you encourage them to offer additional non-financial compensation to woo you. Use the formula at the end of this chapter to determine what you think you are worth, then use that figure as the central point of your range.

2) Giving a specific figure.

When answering the interviewer's question about your salary requirements, you could respond with a specific dollar figure. Such a practice generally limits any negotiation and will generate a response that it is either "in the ball park" or out of the range they were considering for the position. In the former case, the interviewing process will continue. On the other hand, if your requirements are way out of their range, the interview will usually be terminated.

If you tell the employer that you need $X0,000 per year to cover your expenses, you will most likely not find a sympathetic ear. The employer is not as concerned about your expenses as he is about what you can do for the company. You have to prove that you are worth every penny of that amount in long-term value to the company. Any figure could seem high if you have not had the chance to demonstrate the benefits that command it. If the question of salary comes up before you have had time to do so, try to delay your response until you have established sufficient value for yourself.

Value-added pricing.

Whether you give a range or a specific amount, you should have a minimum figure in mind, rounded off to the next highest thousand-dollar level. Further, you should have solid reasoning to explain how you arrived at it. And you should be able to justify your request with facts to prove your potential value to the company.

An explanation of your worth will help you avoid taking simply whatever the employer offers. That could lead to an unhappy experience at best or to more serious consequences, such as financial ruin. Your income should provide you with a comfortable existence so your thoughts and energy can be applied to job performance. If not, you need to cut your costs or increase your income by providing more benefits, either to your current employer or a new one.

If you want to determine the correct price for your services, you should begin by determining your total living expenses. Exhibit 7 shows a sample cash-flow analysis. Use this or a similar form to calculate your needs. Such an analysis will also point out areas in which you can cut expenses. If you have variable costs that have high peaks and valleys, this form will also indicate the impact of these on your budget. And it will show you how much room you have for negotiating non-wage compensation.

This analysis assumes you have $1000 in your saving's account on the first day of January. When you add your salary for that month, your total cash available for January is $3175. When you deduct your expenses from that amount, you have $964 left over with which to begin February. The beginning cash for each month is the cash remaining after all your expenses are paid for the previous month.

EXHIBIT 7: SAMPLE CASH-FLOW ANALYSIS

	JAN	FEB	MAR	APR	MAY	JUN	JUL	AUG	SEP	OCT	NOV	DEC	TOTAL
CASH AVAILABLE													
Beginning Cash	$1000	$964	$949	$902	$854	$730	$600	$475	$400	$331	$261	$197	$7661
Income	2175	2175	2175	2175	2175	2175	2175	2175	2175	2175	2175	2175	26100
Total Cash Available	**3175**	**3139**	**3124**	**3077**	**3029**	**2905**	**2775**	**2650**	**2575**	**2506**	**2439**	**2372**	**33761**
FIXED COSTS													
Housing	800	800	800	800	800	800	800	800	800	800	800	800	9600
School Loan	125	125	125	125	125	125	125	125	125	125	125	125	1500
Car Payment	290	290	290	290	290	290	290	290	290	290	290	290	3480
Car Insurance	150	150	150	150	150	150	150	150	150	150	150	150	1800
Medical Insurance	85	85	85	85	85	85	85	85	85	85	85	85	1020
Gym	50	50	50	50	50	50	50	50	50	50	50	50	600
Total Fixed Costs	**1500**	**1500**	**1500**	**1500**	**1500**	**1500**	**1500**	**1500**	**1500**	**1500**	**1500**	**1500**	**18000**
VARIABLE COSTS													
Sears	20	25	25	25	25	30	30	25	25	25	20	20	295
Visa	35	35	50	50	50	50	45	45	45	45	45	45	540
Food	315	290	290	290	360	360	360	320	320	320	320	320	3865
Phone	25	25	35	35	35	30	30	30	30	30	30	30	365
Utilities	50	50	45	45	45	55	55	55	50	50	50	50	600
Gas(Car)	20	20	30	30	30	25	25	25	25	25	25	25	305
Misc	47	45	48	48	55	55	55	50	50	50	49	49	597
Total Variable Costs	**512**	**490**	**523**	**523**	**600**	**605**	**600**	**550**	**545**	**545**	**539**	**539**	**6567**
SAVINGS	200	200	200	200	200	200	200	200	200	200	200	200	2400
TOTAL COSTS	2212	2190	2223	2223	2300	2305	2300	2250	2245	2245	2239	2239	$26967
ENDING CASH	$964	$949	$902	$854	$730	$600	$475	$400	$331	$261	$197	$133	

As Exhibit 7 illustrates, your fixed costs (rent, car payments, insurance, etc) could be $1500 per month, and your variable costs could be $500 or more. It also assumes you want to save $200 per month. Your total monthly costs could be more than $2,200. You can still cover your total expenses in the example, assuming you are starting with $1000 in your account.

Manipulate this data to yield additional valuable information. For example, if you know your break-even income, you'll be able to pinpoint the income you need more accurately. The chart below shows you how to combine the decision factors you control with those elements that are not under your control.

Annual Net Income	Monthly Income	Fixed Costs	Variable Costs	Desired Savings	Probability Factor	Discretionary Income
$20,000	$1,667	$1500	$500	$200	1.0	($533)
25,000	2,083	1500	500	200	.9	(117)
30,000	2,500	1500	500	200	.8	320
35,000	2,917	1500	500	200	.6	430
40,000	3,333	1500	500	200	.5	567
45,000	3,750	1500	500	200	.4	620
50,000	4,167	1500	500	200	.3	590
55,000	4,583	1500	500	200	.1	238

The column headed "Probability Factor" takes into consideration the external environment. It represents the likelihood of achieving the annual net salary shown at the left. You have to determine these figures based on "gut feel" or from your experience so far in your job search.

For example, a penetration-pricing strategy could set your <u>net</u> income at $20,000 a year (don't forget to compensate for taxes and other deductions). You are certain you could sell yourself for this amount (100% probability). However, at this income you'd cover your fixed costs but not have enough to cover all your variable costs and savings.

On the other hand, a skimming strategy would establish your price at $45,000 per year. You could maximize your discretionary income, but the likelihood of your getting that much money is only about 40%. It may be worth trying for that if you are currently employed (i.e. have income to sustain yourself while you wait for the right opportunity) and can demonstrate that you are worth that much.

Thus, given your present total costs and need to save $200 per month, you have to secure a position paying (after deductions) of $26,100 per year, or $2,175 per month (your break even point). The probability of this happening would be about 80%.

You could stop here and go out into the market asking for a starting salary that would net a paycheck of $2175 per month. You would be happy for a while but as Exhibit 7 shows, your cash at the beginning of each month is dwindling rather quickly. By the end of the year, you'll start to feel the pressure of making ends meet, assuming no extraordinary events occur during that time.

But here is where all your research will pay off. You can customize your pricing strategy to incorporate all the unique benefits you have to offer, geographical considerations or any factors that will affect your income and expenses.

The formula below shows you how to maximize your income by providing for all the individual circumstances of your specific job search. It is based on <u>costs</u> but allows consideration for the benefits you offer. The only quantifiable elements of the equation are expenses, savings and perhaps cost of living differences. The other elements need to be qualified by your individual circumstances and objectives.

Use the equation below to get a good feel for what you are worth. When the interviewer asks you "What are your salary requirements?," you'll have a specific answer (or the center point for your range) and the data to substantiate your request. The interviewer may not agree with the total amount, but if you have a reasonable argument for the income you require, you will be in a much better position to negotiate. The equation and an example of how it may be used are found below.

PRICE = GROSS INCOME TO COVER EXPENSES + SAVINGS + UNIQUE BENEFITS ± MARKET CONDITIONS ± COMPETITIVE CONDITIONS + SPECIAL ABILITIES ± COST OF LIVING ± PSYCHIC INCOME ± EDUCATION

Once you are further along in your career, you could replace the gross income element in the formula. In its place you would substitute your market value at the present time. This could be what you are currently making or what you think your skills are worth. A new formula would look like the following:

PRICE = PRESENT MARKET VALUE + SAVINGS + UNIQUE BENEFITS ± MARKET CONDITIONS ± COMPETITIVE CONDITIONS + SPECIAL ABILITIES ± COST OF LIVING ± PSYCHIC INCOME ± EDUCATION

EXAMPLE (USING THE FORMULA BASED ON COSTS):

You just graduated college and your monthly expenses are $2000. You'll need to gross about 30% more than that to take home this amount. You then decide that you need to save another $200 per month in order to buy a house when you get married. You graduated sixth in your class of 500, so you feel that you can demonstrate a 10% premium. The market conditions are in recession, so you'll deduct 5%. Consequently, competitive conditions are more intense, so you'll offer a 5% discount on your skills. You were not a sports hero, and you haven't had the chance to develop any other special abilities, so this item will not affect the formula. You feel that by moving to Los Angeles, you can find employment in your field, but the cost of living will be about 15% more than that which you are used to. You don't feel that your experience at this time warrants any psychic income greater than a basic benefit package. And you have a college degree but no graduate education yet, so no premium is warranted here in the present competitive environment. Your formula would look something like what follows:

$3100 = GROSS INCOME TO COVER EXPENSES ($2600) + SAVINGS (+$200) + UNIQUE BENEFITS (+$260) ± MARKET CONDITIONS (-$130) ± COMPETITIVE CONDITIONS (-$130) + SPECIAL ABILITIES ($0) ± COST OF LIVING (+$390) ± PSYCHIC INCOME ($0) ± EDUCATION ($0)

If you considered only a gross income to cover your monthly expenses, you would price yourself at $2600 per month (or $31,200 per year). When you take other considerations into account, you can calculate an annual salary of $37,080 which translates into a monthly premium of $490, providing you with another $5880 per year. You certainly recouped the cost of Job Search 101.

Once you set a goal for your market value, don't be too quick to stray from this amount. Hold your ground for as long as you feel it is prudent to do so. Explain how you determined this price and what you can bring to the company to justify it. If the company makes a counter offer with a reasonable figure that doesn't compromise your objectives, you have to make the decision whether or not to accept it.

ASSIGNMENTS:

4.1) Create a monthly budget using the format in Exhibit 7. Determine a realistic gross income to cover these expenditures, plus a miscellaneous factor for emergencies.

4.2) Add to this amount weighted factors for each of the considerations presented in the formula. From these calculations, determine your optimum market price.

CHAPTER FIVE

PASS The Word About Your Ability

There are four basic pieces in the marketing puzzle that must be brought together in your career campaign. You already have three of these in place. The benefits of your Product are defined and "improved;" you have set a fair Price for it and have decided on the Place in which you will offer your services for sale. Yet all this work is for naught if you don't Promote and communicate your benefits to the proper target, i.e., the potential employers in need of the unique benefits that you can provide.

The Four Horsemen.

Just as there are four basic pieces in your marketing puzzle, there are four elements at your disposal in promotional strategy. Together they form the acronym **PASS**. The first three of these are considered mass-communication devices. They allow contact with a large number of people in a short amount of time, and they are made operational through non-personal presentation. These are **P**ublicity, **A**dvertising and **S**ales promotion. The fourth element, **S**elling, involves person-to-person communication.

There are significant differences between mass and personal communications, other than the obvious ones. Mass communications are those that reach a large number of people in a relatively short period of time. These will more quickly and broadly announce the fact that you are available and that you have significant benefits to offer. If your benefits are sufficiently different and in demand, mass communications can provide you with an efficient means of promoting yourself. On the other hand, personal communication deals with one-on-one situations where you have the chance to ask and answer questions.

A good promotional strategy utilizes a mixture of all these elements and implements each at the time it will be most effective in your search. As a general rule of thumb, you'll use more of the mass communication techniques (i.e., direct mail) early in your search to generate large numbers of opportunities. Once you have narrowed down this list, you can then initiate a more personal search to contact those who have the highest degree of interest.

In one day you could reach 5000 prospective employers with an advertisement about yourself, perhaps 500 people with a letter, 50 people over the telephone or 5 good personal meetings. As the quantity of people you contact each day decreases, the quality (and cost) of each contact increases.

PASSing The Word:

<u>**Mass Communication**</u>

> **Publicity:** Non-paid and non-personal stimulation of demand for your services; includes involvement in support groups and trade associations, creating newspaper articles, and using testimonials

> **Advertising:** The presentation and promotion of information through non-personal means; includes your resume, cover letter, direct-mail program, etc.

> **Sales promotion:** Short-term incentives designed to stimulate the purchase of your services; includes your career reply card and personal career card

<u>**Personal Communication**</u>

> **Selling:** Persuading prospective employers to hire you through the use of person-to-person presentations; examples include job fairs, cold calls and telephone techniques

The seven keys to successful communications.

The quality of all your contacts will be improved by following certain guidelines. These are the "Seven Cs" of good strategy, and they establish the criteria for effective promotional implementation. These seven standards require that your communication tools be creative, credible, convincing, complete, current, clear and concise.

1) CREATIVE

An important thing to remember about promotional strategy is that there is no "one way" to do any of it. Of course there are certain things that are expected of you (a resume, for example). But you can express your individualism and creativity in a job search and still maintain a professional image.

Too many people think creativity means an outlandish departure from conventional techniques. But it doesn't have to be so extreme. Since you have control over your promotional efforts, you should utilize inventive techniques to make yourself stand out professionally among your competitors.

With this in mind, any communication you have with a potential employer must be professional as well individual. Promotional strategies are meant to present your capabilities and benefits in the most positive, business-like, yet appropriately innovative manner possible. Your career specialty or personality may demand a more traditional approach, and this is fine. Apply the information given here as you see fit in your particular circumstances.

I've had people send me resumes printed on paper in the shape of a hand to "give me a hand" with my sales efforts. Another came in the shape of a foot, to "get his foot in the door." These approaches do not make you conspicuous in a positive way. Creativity will better serve your campaign if it is applied to demonstrate your ability to find innovative and successful approaches to solving a problem.

Prove your problem-solving skills.

One factor in your candidacy that will help distinguish you from your competition is your ability to prove that you can take existing information and apply it in a unique way. If you can demonstrate that you can solve a problem with creativity, you'll be considered a valuable employee. You don't have to come up with a radically new idea in order to be successful. Sometimes it can be just a slight change from something that is already being done.

Confessions of a problem solver.

For example, there was one company with which I was particularly interested in working. They were well known in the healthcare field, and I knew several of their distributors and customers. I contacted these and told them I was calling for information to help me in an interview.

In the process, I uncovered several new concepts that could make my target company more successful in motivating their distributors' sales people. I called my target company's marketing manager and told him I had a few ideas for communicating with their distributors to help make them better informed. He gave me an appointment, and I showed him my ideas.

They were already sending out a newsletter to their distributors, but the information was not in a form that was useful to their sales force. Since these people spent many hours a day driving, they had little time to read the newsletter. I made the recommendation that they send out the same information but with several additional headings that would prove beneficial. However, I told him that if they sent the newsletter out as an audio cassette, it would be much more useful. The sales people could listen to the cassettes while driving. When they needed a "refresher" later, they could always re-listen to the information. I was offered the job to implement this program, and it was an enormous success.

Creative solutions to problems are born out of necessity. During your search, you'll be faced with many obstacles that will require innovative ways to hurdle them. As you look for different and better ways to surmount them, you'll stretch your imagination and the solutions will come to you.

The 20 questions in Chapter 12 are designed to stimulate your creativity in your job search. Use that information to help design new approaches to your quest and to the ways in which you communicate these to a prospective employer.

2) CREDIBLE.

Always keep in mind that in order for your self-promotion to be taken seriously, your promotional devices cannot be so outlandish as to reduce their credibility. Even though something is true, it is not always believable. It may be true that your actions increased your territory's annual sales by 500%. But an interviewer may listen to this with his tongue in his cheek unless you can provide third-party testimonials, letters from your customers or whatever it takes to document this statement.

You can also demonstrate credibility by effectively using the specific vocabulary of an industry. It is important to let the interviewer know that you understand the basic jargon of the market and can intelligently hold a conversation with him. As you do this, your credibility will be enhanced.

You can damage your credibility with inconsistent statements. You may say that you are a hard worker, but a 2.5 grade-point average may not substantiate that. Don't overstate or understate your accomplishments and keep them all consistent with the true image of yourself.

Credibility is also honesty. Don't ever misrepresent yourself on a resume or during an interview. It will always come back to haunt you, and once credibility is lost, it is difficult to re-establish.

3) CONVINCING

In order for your promotional program to be convincing, it must document the truth in a persuasive manner. Proving what you say can be particularly important. Your cover letter and resume should provide enough details of your accomplishments to convince the reader to call you for an interview. Provide and substantiate the reasons why you would make a better employee than any other candidate.

4) COMPLETE

The objective of your correspondence is to help you obtain an interview. If you tell too much, or not enough, you can reduce the chances of this happening. Present the primary benefits that are important to your current target company; then leave the remaining information to be told during the interview itself.

You shouldn't tell your entire life story in your resume or other correspondence. For a particular position, provide only the information needed to land that specific job without being misleading. Do not intentionally omit important information. Your correspondence must be complete without the errors of omission or commission.

If you insist on giving a detailed account of your background and interests in every piece of your correspondence, you may annoy the interviewer with extraneous facts that he or she considers a waste of time. Tell what is necessary and leave the explanations for later in the process.

5) CURRENT

Similarly, your communication must be current. Keep your Career Journal up to date with details of important events as they occur to you or as a result of your efforts. It may be your inauguration into the local Chamber of Commerce or that you were a guest speaker at the local American Marketing Association meeting. Review this list regularly, and use the information contained therein as you feel it is strategically appropriate.

Remain informed on current events. Read newspapers and listen to or watch the news reports so you can initiate or respond to conversational questions about late-breaking stories. Always review the recent business sections of your local newspaper for examples to use during your interview or in your correspondence.

6) CLEAR

Your promotional pieces will be ineffective if their execution is not clear. Your communication device is not the place to use big words just for the sake of impressing someone. Instead, use this opportunity to demonstrate your grasp of proper grammar and organization. Use short sentences and words. Use "white space" in your letters and resume. Make your correspondence look inviting to read. Then lead the reader through each benefit-packed paragraph to a clearly defined call to action.

Clarity will also minimize distortion of your intended message. Your intent may be perfectly clear to you, but it may be misinterpreted by the listener. For example, if you say you're a hard worker, what does that mean to the interviewer? It could be construed that you put in a full day's work, perhaps from "9 to 5." On the other hand, it might be interpreted as your doing only what you are told to do. Always follow your statement with examples that prove the impression you want to make. Then ask questions to make sure your intended message was the one that was actually received.

7) CONCISE

Your message should always be to the point. Don't waste the reader's time by warming up with extraneous information. Consider the environment in which the person is reading your message. If the prospective employer has just received 500 cover letters and resumes, she cannot afford the time to read anything that is not germane to the decision at hand.

Be succinct and present your benefits as they relate to the requirements sought for that particular position. There is a quotation that bears upon this situation:

**Tell me quick, and tell me true,
or else my friend, the heck with you.**

Keep this in mind as you attempt to persuade someone to hire you, whether you are doing it in person or through one of the non-personal means.

These are all learned traits, and the more you practice them, the better you will become in their use. Write a cover letter, then critically evaluate it. Is there a more creative way of getting your point across? Did you offer proof for a statement that could be misconstrued? Did you list all the pertinent benefits you can provide a company? Are there any events that occurred since your last writing that would be applicable to your campaign? Does it look inviting to read? Were you succinct in your commentary? Apply these standards, make necessary revisions, and then put the letter down for a few days. When you come back to it, you'll have a fresh perspective and new ideas to improve it.

PASS with the Seven Cs.

You can apply the Seven "Cs" in all your mass and personal communications. Use them in letters, during your interviews, on the telephone and in every applicable situation. Practice using them with your friends, relatives and in all aspects of your career search. As you review the advertising, sales promotion, public relations and personal selling strategies presented in the remainder of this book, think of how you can utilize the Seven "Cs" to customize them to your personality and needs.

MASS COMMUNICATION

1) Advertising

The mainstay in Phase One of your career search is the package you send to a prospective employer that includes your cover letter and resume. Ironically, these two pieces cause the demise of many applicants' candidacies before they even learn the name of the company receiving them.

A successful cover letter and resume must communicate to the reader that you can benefit the company more than your competitors can, and because of that fact they should interview you. Therefore, it must be written with an understanding of the reader's point of view and with an awareness of the conditions under which they will be read. The purpose is to make you stand out among your competitors professionally and motivate the reader to invite you to come in for a personal interview.

Take the reader's perspective.

For a moment, put yourself in the position of a potential employer who has recently placed an advertisement in the classified section of your local Sunday newspaper. By Tuesday or Wednesday, the advertiser receives between 0 and 1000 or more cover-letter/resume packages, in addition to interruptions for phone calls from applicants and head hunters, plus an occasional FAX'd resume. The company representative knows he or she cannot interview all these people, and experience has shown that many are not adequately qualified anyway. With this in mind, the reader begins the task of reading the cover letters and resumes, weeding out those who will not survive the first cut.

The prospective employer will make space on his desk for three piles. Eventually one will contain those resumes that will not be considered, one will be for those that have possibilities, and the third (and smallest) will contain resumes for those candidates who will be given additional consideration. To further complicate matters, the individual reading your package may not even be the decision maker. He or she may be a personnel person whose job it is to provide the decision maker with a recommendation of those applicants to pursue.

Many factors cause a package to be placed in the first pile, eliminating the candidate from receiving any further attention. If the initial impression of the cover letter is unfavorable, it is unlikely that the resume will be seriously examined. A negative first impression could be caused by a letter that is a bad Xerox copy, contains spelling errors, or has fingerprints or smudges on it from the carbon paper or typewriter ribbon. And once he begins reading, your sentence structure and vocabulary continue building either a positive or negative image of you.

Into this first pile will also go the FAX'd copies that are unreadable, letters printed on florescent paper and even well-written packages from people who are not qualified for the position. You should remember that the reader is going through each and every package, looking for a reason to eliminate that candidate. As soon as a reasonable excuse to eliminate one occurs, it is placed in this pile.

If the first reading shows a candidate has possibilities, it is placed in the second pile. Unless a package is overwhelmingly attractive (as far as presentation and content go), the first pass usually nets only two piles.

Following the first pass through the packages, the applicants in the first pile are sent rejection letters. The remaining stack is again perused, and more candidates are eliminated or placed in the pile for further consideration. As the reader becomes more familiar with the credentials of the applicants, it becomes easier to weed out those that do not warrant further consideration. Those are discarded and sent rejection letters. Others which appear to represent qualified people are placed in the last pile. After a final review, a list is made of those who will either be interviewed over the phone or called in for a personal interview.

Up to this point, you are not thought of as a person. Your cover letter and resume represent the unseen candidate, so it is easier for someone to reject you. The reader has no idea who you are, what a good person you are or what your life's situation is. He doesn't care, because at this point he needs to eliminate those he thinks will not perform on the job as competently as someone else represented in the stack of letters and resumes.

Your package is not read in isolation but in relation to your competitors. If applicants less qualified than you present their backgrounds in a way that makes them seem more suited to the opportunity, they will get the calls. You will get a nicely written letter that your resume will be kept on file for six months should something more suitable come up.

Your cover letter and resume are reviewed in your absence, without giving you the benefit of clarifying any misunderstandings. Therefore, you must follow them up if you are rejected. Ask the interviewer why you were not accepted. If there was a misunderstanding, you should clear it up and re-write your resume to prevent it from happening again.

MAKING A GOOD FIRST IMPRESSION: YOUR COVER LETTER

This process may not seem fair, but it or some similar sequence is used to weed out those who will not be considered. Your cover letter should be properly and persuasively written. If it does not generate a positive feeling in the reader, your resume may be given only a cursory glance, and your package will be placed in the first pile. The objective of your cover letter is to make a favorable impression and create sufficient interest for the reader to review your resume at least with an open mind and at best with positive anticipation.

The proper beginning.

Make sure you show your return address and telephone number. Make it as easy as possible for the interviewer to get in touch with you. Include your home address and telephone number and your school address and telephone number if you want to receive your mail there. Then date the letter.

The recipient's name and the way you write it are important. You'll regularly see ads asking you to respond to a name such as "J. Smith." If this is the case, don't address it as "Mr. J. Smith" or "Ms. J. Smith." At some point you will be wrong, and you will start off with one point deducted from your interview "grade." Address it as J. Smith, XYZ Company, etc. The salutation would then read "Dear J. Smith:."

The same situation applies to names that could belong to either a man or a woman (Chris,

Pat, etc.). If you are to respond to Pat Smith, don't address it to "Mr. Smith" or "Ms. Smith." Use appropriate titles when they are known. If you are asked to respond to Susan Jones, Ph.D., the salutation should read "Dear Dr. Jones:." If you are asked to respond to a medical doctor, address the letter and envelope to Edward Smith, M.D., but the salutation should read "Dear Dr. Smith." If you don't have a person's name to whom you should address the letter, the greeting could read "Dear Executive:." Similarly, if instructed to send the information to the Personnel Director, without a name, your salutation should read "Dear Personnel Director:."

Always make sure you have spelled the recipient's name properly. My spelling of the name "Jud" is obviously with one "d" at the end. This is not the normal way to spell it, and most people add a second "d." I've come to expect that people will misspell it, so when a person spells my name correctly, he makes a favorable impression. Most people are proud of their names, and your misspelling could be considered offensive. Check to see if the name is spelled "Smith" or "Smyth," "Louis" or "Lewis." A misspelled name may not eliminate you as a candidate, but then again, maybe it will.

Frequently you'll be asked to respond to a "blind" ad, one that asks you to send your letter to either an address or a post-office box without a person's name. If you are still employed, you may not want your current employer to receive your resume. Some newspapers have a confidential service and, at your request, will not forward your resume to a specified company.

Writing your letter.

Since the reader is looking for a way to eliminate you as a candidate, you should immediately get his attention in a positive way and then keep him reading by generating additional reasons to do so. Therefore, it is vital to break through the reader's preoccupation barrier and get him to read your letter carefully.

These objectives can be accomplished with a formula used in writing persuasive communications. It is the **AIDA** formula (Attention-Interest-Desire-Action) and is used to create a pathway for the reader to follow through your letter. After getting the reader's attention, each subsequent step should increase the reader's interest and desire to read your resume. At the same time, you should demonstrate that you have the background to succeed in this position and you warrant further consideration. You then end the letter with a request that some positive action take place.

1) The first paragraph: getting attention.

In advertising, it has been proven that five times as many people read the headline than read the copy of an ad. And each succeeding paragraph has progressively fewer and fewer readers. If you want people to review all your information, you have to give them reasons to do so. Consequently, you should implement the guidelines copywriters use to get the attention of readers and lure them into the body text. You can apply the same general principles when writing the first paragraph of your cover letter.

Begin your letter with an Attention-getting statement. Demonstrate that you have read the requirements sought in the ad, you are familiar with the company and you feel that your qualifications are well suited for the position. The first paragraph should be a one or two sentence description of your major benefit and why you feel it would significantly behoove the company to interview you.

Here are several guidelines for your opening statements.

1) Make an immediate, positive impact on the reader:

"I have been the top-rated salesman in each of the last three years. I can do the same for your company."

2) Appeal to the reader's self-interest (i.e., what the classified ad indicated was important for success in the position):

"The requirements sought in your ad closely match the skills I have to offer in ...."

3) Avoid bragging about your capabilities, especially at a competitor's expense. <u>Don't</u> begin:

"No matter how long you search, you won't find a better qualified person than I am for this position."

4) Inject "news" or a feeling of current information:

"As a recently inducted member of the Phi Beta Kappa honor society, I feel that I have the ability to ...."

5) Include the reader's name in the first sentence to get his attention. People are attracted to their own name:

"After reading your ad in the paper, Mr. Balestro, I sincerely feel that I have a great deal to offer your company. For example...."

6) Make it easy to understand. Don't make the reader spend time trying to figure out what you are saying:

"I am a recent college graduate seeking an entry-level position in computer programming."

7) Coordinate it with the other elements in your letter and resume. Don't use an attention-getting headline technique, then revert back to a "ho-hum" style in your body copy.

8) Be specific and to the point. Don't be so general that your benefit could be applied to any company in any situation:

"I have two years of accounting experience in the automotive after-market. I can help your company...."

2) The second paragraph: stimulating interest.

Begin succeeding paragraphs with a "bridge," a word that creates curiosity or gives the reader a reason to continue reading. Examples of bridging words are "Furthermore, consequently, on the other hand, similarly, for example." You should also use the word "you" frequently. It makes the reader think you are writing a personal letter, and he will remain more interested in it. Similarly, you should not refer to yourself in the third person ("he demonstrated...").

Your second paragraph should generate Interest by expanding on your initial benefit statement (the statement of your <u>primary</u> benefit in that situation) and then leading into additional benefits. Describe the results and accomplishments you demonstrated in the past and why you are certain these could be translated to future success at that particular company.

The recently inducted member of Phi Beta Kappa could begin his second paragraph by writing:

> **Subsequently, I have demonstrated my scholastic aptitude by applying textbook information to practical situations. For example ....**

Or the applicant writing Mr. Balestro might continue:

> **In addition, Mr. Balestro, I have demonstrated other skills in the field of creative package design. These include....**

3) Third and fourth paragraphs: building the desire to continue.

You can create **Desire** by adding relevant secondary benefits, and a "grabber" if it applies. Show that you know something about the company and its products. Specifically mention the success you have demonstrated with similar products in the past and how you can translate that into future success with this company. You are selling "potential" at this point, not the past.

In marketing terms, a product can be defined in four ways. <u>The Generic Product</u> is a description of what it is (**I am a college graduate seeking employment**). The <u>Expected Product</u> says that it does what you expect that it would (**I successfully completed all required courses for a Bachelor of Science Degree in Marketing**). The <u>Augmented Product</u> proves that it is worthy of additional consideration because it is better than competing products for some reason (**I successfully applied the principles of marketing and subsequently increased readership of the college newspaper by 54% in two years**). And the <u>Potential Product</u> defines what future possibilities the product could provide (**These same skills will be valuable in helping me increase sales for XYZ Company**). Generate desire among your readers by selling the potential aspects of your product.

Use action- and results-oriented words and phrases.

The words you use to present your credentials are critical. First of all, use action words. Say how you "researched, planned and introduced, demonstrated or created" in your position. Then generate a feeling of enthusiasm for your work by using simple, action-oriented words whenever you can. Create factual, concrete, positive statements that carry a powerful message and convey the concepts of gain or performance in every sentence. And always follow these words with the **accomplishments** that resulted from their use.

Exhibit 8 lists four columns of words. These are designed to help you create phrases that will paint a positive image of your accomplishments. You can use this information to create a four-word phrase beginning with one adverb, then choosing a verb, adjective and noun. This chart is not designed to be read across, so you can mix and match words among the columns. Don't overdo your use of the adverbs, and every phrase does not have to be four words. Carefully pick and choose from among these words to create a few pertinent phrases that describe your particular talents. Of course you aren't limited to these words; seek those that create an accurate and positive word picture of you.

Radio announcers offer an excellent example of creating word pictures. They have to explain what is going on during a sporting event, since you obviously can't see it. On the other hand, if you watch the same event on television, the announcers don't have to create any pictures for you verbally because you can see what is happening. Listen to a good radio commentator describe an event, and you'll have a good example of how to create a positive visual image of yourself.

EXHIBIT 8: WORD FINDERS

ADVERB	VERB	ADJECTIVE	NOUN
Actively	Completed	Significant	Success
Seriously	Continued	Scholastic	Achievement
Consistently	Assured	Competitive	Tenacity
Regularly	Performed	Gratifying	Determination
Quarterly	Attained	Substantial	Skills
Competitively	Achieved	Financial	Attitude
Skillfully	Earned	Enterprising	Nature
Creatively	Strengthened	Leadership	Maturity
Significantly	Excelled	Meaningful	Ability
Instinctively	Enhanced	Learning	Experience
Eagerly	Practiced	Motivational	Flexibility
Enthusiastically	Innovated	Interactive	Communications
Rapidly	Created	Continual	Budget
Ultimately	Developed	Extreme	Tasks
Vigorously	Prepared	Practical	Proficiency
Sensibly	Planned	Solid	Consistency
Systematically	Organized	Lasting	Excellence
Cautiously	Motivated	Technological	Strength
Independently	Increased	Difficult	Knowledge
Confidently	Hired	Consistent	Expertise
Prudently	Convinced	Momentous	Competence
Aggressively	Discovered	Unparalleled	Fitness
Notably	Enjoyed	Noteworthy	Suitability
Extremely	Secured	Praise-worthy	Superiority
Economically	Encouraged	Distinguished	Supremacy
Acutely	Insured	Skillful	Capabilities
Sufficiently	Overcame	Developmental	Studies
Satisfactorily	Acted	Expert	Ideas
Solidly	Accumulated	Complex	Contests
Shrewdly	Mastered	Compound	Challenges
Evidently	Composed	Athletic	Crises
Entirely	Combined	Difficult	Proficiency
Completely	Fulfilled	Successful	Opportunities
Wisely	Participated	Fundamental	Costs
Responsively	Managed	Powerful	Classifications
Quickly	Established	Costly	Expenditures
Permanently	Conducted	Annual	Independence
Sincerely	Succeeded	Sturdy	Optimism
Partially	Accomplished	Aggressive	Enthusiasm
Formally	Offered	Extraordinary	Self-confidence
Wholeheartedly	Displayed	Numerous	Framework
Gradually	Exhibited	Increasing	Environment
Measurably	Proved	Uncommon	Subordinates
Distinctly	Improved	Academic	Managers
Properly	Designed	Collegiate	Members
Naturally	Trained	Healthy	Funds
Overwhelmingly	Supervised	Available	Excitement
Convincingly	Implemented	Genuine	Excess
Distinctly	Invented	Intense	Disorder
Prominently	Sold	Constant	Departments
Duly	Expanded	Momentary	Companies
Habitually	Negotiated	Turbulent	Organizations
Uniformly	Analyzed	Considerable	Committees
Studiously	Reduced	Ordinary	Classes

4) *The closing paragraph*: "closing" the sale.

Finally, the Action paragraph suggests to the reader what the logical next step should be. Do this by summarizing your benefits and asking the reader to continue on to your resume to find out more details about your benefits.

For instance, you could ask the recipient to read your attached resume for more examples of your benefits and accomplishments. If appropriate, you could say that you will call at some date in the future to answer any questions or to set up an interview (be specific about when you will follow up). If you send your letter to a post-office box, you could close with a summary and then a statement that you are looking forward to hearing from them to set up a time to discuss this opportunity personally. Exhibit 9 is an example of such a letter.

Additional details.

Keep several letters on file and use them as the basic outline for a response. Then tailor each letter to the specific qualifications sought for that particular position. Exhibits 9 and 10 serve as examples of such letters. Each describes the benefits provided to previous employers, but using the terms the advertiser described in the ad. Present your benefits in terms that are important to the reader. If the company is seeking an experienced sales manager capable of building a national sales organization, your cover letter should stress your experience in that area. You would not mention that, for example, you worked in telemarketing for a local company selling magazines subscriptions.

EXHIBIT 9: COVER LETTER FOR A RESUME SENT IN RESPONSE TO A BLIND AD

Dear Executive:

I am a proven business professional with more than fifteen years of successful sales and management experience. My sales force recently surpassed corporate objectives by 63%. I am confident that I can apply these skills to your company's long-term benefit as your National Sales Manager.

Furthermore, my experience as Director of Sales has helped me hone my problem-solving skills, as well as my abilities in strategic planning, competitive strategy and marketing through distribution networks. Another position as District Sales Manager enabled me to develop my skills in hiring, developing, and motivating people, as well as working effectively in a teamwork environment.

Time and again I have demonstrated the personal attributes that will lead to my success as your National Sales Manager. These include personal motivation, leadership, diplomacy, determination, creativity and an entrepreneurial and competitive attitude.

My income has increased regularly, with an income of $XX,000 in 1988, $XY,000 in 1989, culminating in a 1990 income of $XZ,000 (including commissions). Annual increases prior to 1988 generally exceeded $X,000.

Please allow me the opportunity to demonstrate my skills to you in a personal interview. I am confident that I could make an immediate and valuable contribution to the achievement of your company's long-term goals. I am looking forward to hearing from you. Thank you.

When you respond with a cover letter, personalize it whenever possible. You obviously can't do this with a letter sent to a post-office box but can under other conditions. Use the person's name and the title of the position and refer to the company's name as frequently as possible. Exhibit 10 shows how a similar letter can be better directed toward an individual and company, when both are known.

EXHIBIT 10: PERSONALIZED COVER LETTER

Mr. Bruce Bradshaw
Creative Communications
711 Gamble Street
Jackson Hole, WY 81234

Dear Mr. Bradshaw:

I have competed against Creative Communications several times during my ten years of selling these services. I have always found your company to be a formidable competitor. I now welcome the opportunity to work for you as your Vice President, Sales.

In testimony to this, my experience as National Sales Manager enabled me to develop my skills in hiring, directing and motivating people to the point where my team surpassed corporate revenue objectives by 28% over each of the past three years. A recent position as Director of Marketing has helped me hone my competitive strategy and problem-solving skills, as well as my abilities in creating sales-support materials and marketing through a distribution network.

Furthermore, Mr. Bradshaw, I have demonstrated the personal attributes that will lead to my success as your Vice President, Sales. These include personal motivation, leadership, determination, creativity and an entrepreneurial and competitive attitude.

In summary, I have regularly surpassed expectations by building and motivating a professional, national sales team and strategically directing their success. Additional accomplishments are summarized in the attached resume.

I am looking forward to the opportunity to discuss my techniques with you in a personal interview. I will call you on February 8th to arrange a time for us to meet. I am confident that I could make an immediate and valuable contribution to the achievement of Creative Communications' long-term goals. Thank you for your consideration.

By changing the order of the job titles you have held, you can lead with the one that is most appropriate to the position at hand. You need not keep these in chronological order in your cover letter as long as you do so in your resume. Just stress the functions and accomplishments that will create value for you in the subject position. And since you know the recipient's name and address, you can find out his telephone number and take the initiative by calling him.

Make sure you show the job title for which you are applying. The company may have different ads running in different papers around the country, each seeking people for a separate job title. If you don't state the position in which you are interested, they will make the choice for you.

Your cover letter should not repeat everything that is in your resume, but it should personalize that information and make it relevant to the specific company to which you are responding. Its objective is to provide the recipient with a reason to read your resume with a degree of positive anticipation. Try to respond to the qualifications they seek in the ad, but don't make excessive use of their words to do so. Say the same thing, using different words at different times.

If the company seeks **leadership skills**, you can say that you have experience

- Leading organized groups
- Effectively directing others
- Motivating individuals
- Taking acceptable risks

- Making difficult decisions
- Gaining others' cooperation
- Facilitating change
- Winning others' confidence

If the company seeks **management skills**, you can say that you have experience

- Forming objectives
- Managing time and energy
- Delegating responsibility
- Anticipating future needs

- Building teamwork
- Delegating authority
- Coping with ambiguity
- Establishing priorities

If the company seeks **general communications skills**, you can say that you have experience

- Probing for need
- Listening effectively
- Writing convincingly
- Speaking persuasively

- Explaining concepts well
- Reading comprehensively
- Reporting accurately
- Writing concisely

A concept called the "Halo Effect" may have a bearing on your success in landing a job offer. Briefly, this theory states that people generally judge others favorably or unfavorably on the basis of one strong or weak point, respectively. If your cover letter creates a good overall impression of you, your resume is more likely to be favorably assessed, and vice versa. The reader will seek information in your resume that will confirm her pre-conception, and you will either move to the next step or be added to the list of those who will receive a rejection letter.

Not every ad requests a salary history. It is not in your best interests to provide this information too early in the process. You should delay any discussion of income until you have had the chance to create sufficient value for your services. Any salary is too much if the prospective employer has no idea what benefits you offer for that amount. If a salary history is not requested, delete that information from your cover letter. In the same case, if you have a separate salary history on a separate page omit that from your response package.

Customizing your cover letter.

If you are using a typewriter, there are ways to create individual cover letters without spending hours of your Sundays typing them. First of all, you can create two or three different cover letters, leaving room for the address and salutation. Close the letters with a sentence that may be concluded with the company's name. For example, you could end the last paragraph with the sentence "I am confident that I could make a valuable contribution to the long-term goals of (blank)." Have these printed, and then when the time comes to respond to an ad, simply type in the address and salutation and then the company's name at the end.

You may find yourself sending out only a few resumes a week. If this is the case, you can type each cover letter as an original. Take your time, and don't try to type more than two or three without taking a break. By the time you get to the third or fourth letter, you may find yourself typing too quickly and making mistakes. A letter with "white-out" spots on it doesn't look good, and the individual letters re-typed over correction fluid are never as crisp as the others.

If you have access to a word processor, it is much easier to customize a cover letter. Keep several different ones on file, and add specific details to each response. Just be careful to make all the changes in each letter. For example, you may change the salutation to "Dear Mr. Loudermilk:" but forget to change the reference to the previous addressee in the body text.

Reproducing your cover letter.

Your cover letter should be individually typed on 8 1/2" x 11" paper that matches that of your resume. Use a good quality paper, with matching envelopes. And it should be typed using proper business format.

When you have your cover letter printed, use all the capabilities the printer has to offer. For example, you can use different color inks to highlight certain parts of your letter. You could use black ink except for your benefit statements, which you could have printed in red. Or perhaps reproduce your accomplishments in blue or another color. It is also acceptable to hand write a P.S., using a different color ink, thus tailoring a pre-printed letter to an individual reader's needs. Signing a letter in a different color ink has proven to increase the response rate for direct-mail letters and may translate into increased readership of your resume.

Assuming the reader is interested in continuing, he will turn the page to your resume. It is critical to keep the momentum going and not let the interest and desire wane. The reader is thinking, "OK, now you've got me interested. Let's see you prove it."

TELLING YOUR STORY: YOUR RESUME

Objective of your resume.

The objective of your resume is to persuade the reader to contact you to come in for a personal interview. Do this by continuing the positive momentum begun in the cover letter and adding complete documentation of your benefits and background. The resume also must look inviting to read, be professionally reproduced and contain results-oriented words and phrases. You don't need to tell every function of every position. But you must describe what you accomplished and how you can translate these achievements to future success for this particular company.

Your resume must be a sequential, benefit-oriented, clearly presented summary of your education and experience, written to entice the reader to invite you in for a personal interview. Far too many resumes present only a job description, and most are no different from the last or next twenty resumes the reader will evaluate. You must stand out professionally among this crowd by following the Feature-Advantage-Benefit sequence.

As you sit down to write your resume, keep your Talent-Analysis Sheet and Self-Analysis Balance Sheet in front of you. Also have a copy of Exhibit 8 (Word Finders), a dictionary and a thesaurus handy. Don't be concerned with the physical layout of the finished resume at this point. Simply set out to communicate the benefits of your background. You want to show how your accomplishments will enable you to function for a prospective employer successfully and achieve your objective.

Helpful writing techniques.

Several methods can help you write more informatively and persuasively. These include the following:

- It's not necessary to use complete sentences.

- Keep the presentation sequence the same for all parts of each paragraph.

- Begin writing broad, general statements. Then reduce these to short, descriptive phrases and sentences. Think of the funnel technique, i.e., go from general to specific copy. Write more than you need, then begin to edit out unnecessary information.

- Use the **PREP** formula. Make a **P**oint, give a **R**eason for it, then an **E**xample of it. Finally **P**rove your point by making a statement of the benefit or accomplishment.

- Keep your career objective in mind as you write. Use terms that support it.

- Show the reader that the company will be better off hiring you than one of your competitors.

MAJOR HEADINGS.

1) Address.

Make it as easy as possible for the reader to get in touch with you. Clearly show your name, address and telephone number at the top of your resume. Present yourself by the name you ordinarily use in your business life. Spell it out rather than using initials only. Avoid nicknames at this stage. Show your complete address, again spelling out all words, including your city and state. Show your full telephone number and area code, even if you only plan to apply to local employers. Don't assume that because you have this information on your cover letter that there is no need to repeat it on your resume. Many times these two documents become separated, so each should be identifiable on its own.

2) Career Objective.

If you choose to state your career objective, it should appear at the beginning of your resume. A specific objective demonstrates that you know what you want. If you are not absolutely sure what that is, you may want to create separate resumes, each with a different objective. If you choose to do this, don't just change the objective and reprint the remainder of the resume as it was with a different objective. If properly written, your resume should demonstrate that you have the ability to fulfill your specific career objective.

Your objective should be a clear statement of what you want to do with your career. Instead of writing "A recent college graduate seeking an entry-level position in sales," you could change it to feed back the wording in the ad. You could adapt this to read, "A recent college graduate with strong marketing skills seeks a stimulating sales position where creative and persuasive skills may be applied to achieve challenging goals."

Many people don't know exactly what they want in a career. If you are in this category, you may choose to omit the objective statement altogether. But if you have the conviction and determination to reach one objective, place it right at the beginning of your resume, thus weeding out companies that cannot provide the means for you to reach your career goal.

3) Employment experience.

Unless you have graduated from a top-name school, or if you do not have much work experience, you should list your employment highlights right after your objective. If nothing else, you can support your objective through professional achievement. But the ways in which this information is presented will make you stand out from or be part of the crowd. Here's your opportunity to excel.

Your professional experience should be in reverse chronological order, with your current or most recent position shown first. Include all employers and account for your time completely since leaving school or military service. Your competitors will most likely give their company name, job title and job description, which becomes a routine, "ho-hum" presentation that will generate few interviews. The momentum, if any, from the cover letter is lost, as is the opportunity for a new career. An example of this non-motivating job description is as follows:

XYZ Company   1/1/88 - Present

Product Manager: researched, planned and introduced three new products; prepared accurate forecasts and annual plans, and implemented sales-support programs

---

You, on the other hand, have already created the basis for a results-oriented resume. Use the information in your Talent-Analysis Sheet and Self-Analysis Balance Sheet to write the first draft of your resume. Set up a format such as that shown below and fill in the outline. Re-work it until you feel comfortable with it. Then leave it alone for a few days while those in your Brain Trust review it. Then go back to it, with their comments, and write another version. Keep re-writing until you feel satisfied that you have what you want.

Use the structure in Exhibit 11 carefully. It should serve only to help you organize the information with which to write your benefit-oriented resume in motivating terms. It should not serve as the final layout. In your future drafts, use the final layout you have decided upon in place of that shown in Exhibit 11 to create your outline. Don't get locked into one-and-only-one format, or you could be missing an excellent opportunity to excel vis-a-vis your competition.

EXHIBIT 11: RESUME STRUCTURE FOR THE EMPLOYMENT SEGMENT

EXPERIENCE

Dates	Company name
	Job Title; responsibilities; skills developed; accomplishments

Dates   Company name
Job Title; responsibilities; skills developed;
 accomplishments

Dates   Company name
Job Title; responsibilities; skills developed;
accomplishments

Dates   Company name
Job Title; responsibilities; skills developed;
accomplishments

This approach, or whatever structure you finally choose, will provide you with the details to create a result-oriented, persuasive resume that will generate a significantly greater number of job interviews. Instead of the routine job description previously shown, your resume will contain paragraphs with these hard-hitting words:

XYZ Company   1/1/88 - Present
Product Manager: **researched, planned and introduced three new products that captured 19% market share in a competitive environment; generated $3,000,000 in gross revenue (10% of Division total) with high contribution margins; demonstrated my forecasting skills with a plan that achieved 102% of objective.**

---

4) Related experience.

If you have a background in a variety of positions, some may be more relevant to your career objective than others. An excellent way to present these according to their applicability is to show your experience under two headings: 1) Related Experience, and 2) Other Experience.

If, for example, you are seeking a career as a journalist, you should list the positions that would support this objective under Related Experience. Then under the second heading, you would list experience you had working in a restaurant as a waitress/waiter or as a bank clerk.

5) Education.

Your education should follow your employment achievements, again listed in reverse chronological order. Show the names of each school, city, degrees earned, major fields of study and the dates of attendance. It's probably not a good idea to show your GPA if it is below a 3.0.

If you have a college degree, it is not necessary to show the name of your high school. If you don't have a college degree, mention all the schools you have attended and the dates of each.

Your resume should make the most of your educational and extra-curricular activities, particularly if your employment experience is limited. You could prepare a special section called EDUCATIONAL HIGHLIGHTS. Use your favorite subjects or events as subheads, and describe the ways in which you applied your education. An example is shown below:

EDUCATIONAL HIGHLIGHTS

English: Maintained a 3.75 grade average; developed skills in written and oral communication; sharpened my creative ability by writing numerous fiction stories; won an award for the Best Fiction Story in the contest for the college newsletter.

Math: Earned a consistent 3.4 cumulative grade average over four years of progressively more challenging mathematics; demonstrated significant skill by developing my analytical and problem-solving abilities.

Another format for organizing your thinking when writing this section is shown in Exhibit 12, below. The same cautions apply to this as for Exhibit 11.

EXHIBIT 12: RESUME STRUCTURE FOR THE EDUCATION SEGMENT

EDUCATION

Dates   School Name
               Major; degree; Grade Point Average (if over a 3.0); skills developed; accomplishments resulting from the application of this knowledge.

Don't oversell.

You may feel other information is necessary to include in your resume. Seriously consider every additional detail before doing so. Extraneous information can give the reader a more complete picture of you, or it could bring up a question mark or negative point if the reader misinterprets your additional data. If there is something about your background that is an essential adjunct to your career objective, then add it. Some of these questionable subjects include the following:

1) Special Skills.

You may wish to include the names of key professional or trade associations in which you are an active member. Refrain from listing those that could be offensive to some readers. You may want to show your fluency in a foreign language if it is pertinent to your objective.

2) Personal data.

There are two schools of thought about including personal data in your resume. One says it is a good idea; the reader can get a better feel for you as an individual. The other obviously says it is not a good idea because it could create a negative image of you. The latter theory also assumes the reader has so many letters and resumes to read that he is thinking to himself, "Tell me quick and tell me true, or else my friend the heck with you." In this case, too much information may be viewed as a negative.

Regardless of your decision to include this information, people will create a mental picture of you as they read your cover letter and resume. Keep this in mind as you write them. Creating a positive projection of yourself through the use of image-creating words is more effective than simply describing yourself.

For example, there are many different ways a 6'1", 210 pound person could look, and the reader is free to create a positive or negative image in his mind unless otherwise directed. If you skillfully create a mental picture of yourself through positive, success-oriented words, you can favorably manipulate the impression. A simple listing of your height and weight will not contribute as much to your image as will a description of "a competitive athlete with an image that portrays a life-long commitment to physical fitness." Choose your words carefully to create a favorable picture of yourself in the reader's mind. You could do this in the cover letter instead of your resume.

In the final analysis, most personal data is optional. Just be aware of the positive or negative impact it may have. If you choose to indicate your age, showing your birth date will prevent your resume from becoming obsolete after your next birthday. But avoid listing it and your Social Security number, marriage status, number of children and health condition if at all possible.

3) Additional information.

This is not the time or the place to list all the achievements you made as an Eagle Scout, Girl Scout or something else unrelated. The obvious exception is if you are applying for a position with the Boy or Girl Scouts of America. The same general principle applies to hobbies and other activities. Don't add any reference to your salary history on your resume, either.

Creating the physical layout.

Once you have your copy completed, you must decide how to make it look attractive and inviting to read. Try not to use the formats everyone else uses. If you feel more comfortable doing so, then go ahead. But if you want to express your individualism professionally, now is your chance. But whatever you choose, adhere to these basic guidelines:

- Use "white space." White space is the borders and space between paragraphs and sections which give the visual presentation an open, uncluttered look.

- Draw attention to important benefits and accomplishments by using *italics*, <u>underlining</u>, **bold face type**, CAPITAL LETTERS, but don't overuse any one technique.

- Break up the layout with larger type sizes for the headings and through the use of lines to separate different segments.

- Use "bullets" to highlight important topics. The dot at the beginning of each of these sentences is a "bullet."

- Keep your presentation to one page by being brief and using small type sizes. (Don't use a type size smaller than 8 points. 10 to 12 points is best. The text on this page is 12 points.) It is not critical to keep it to one page, but there should be a strong reason for using more than two pages.

- Give emphasis to a specific segment of your background, i.e., experience over education, by giving it a greater proportion of the total space of your resume.

The Functional Resume.

Another resume format has a layout that is different from the reverse-chronological layout. It has been called the Functional Resume, Focused Resume and Targeted Resume. Regardless of what it is called, it emphasizes the functions you have performed and the skills you have developed rather than the employers and positions themselves.

If you have spent many years with one company and have performed a variety of jobs with them, this format would be excellent to use. It is also useful if you have changed industries and are applying for a job that could utilize your generic skills (analytical, persuasive, creative, etc.), rather than specific industry experience. It would also be beneficial for people returning to the work force after a period of unemployment. And those whose work history is not consistent, or who have progressed at a slower than expected pace, will find this to be a good format.

On the other hand, there are three reasons not to use this format. First, some employers immediately suspect this layout as trying to hide something in your background. Second, it can be difficult to show your job progression clearly. And finally, if you have worked for a major company in your field, this fact could remain hidden.

If you decide to use the functional format, follow the same guidelines that apply to the reverse-chronological style. Use action-oriented words and give examples of the accomplishments that you achieved, not just the functions and skills themselves. Point out exactly what it is that you can do for the potential employer by demonstrating that you know what is expected of someone in the position.

After you list your skills and achievements, be sure to include a summary of your jobs, in the order held. Account for all time and show the dates of employment. Also, show your job titles.

Your education should be given the same emphasis you would have otherwise given it. Either place it before or after your work experience. Show the dates, degrees, certificates, grade-point averages, etc., just as you would do with the reverse-chronological format.

A general layout could look something like this:

Name
Address
Telephone Number

Objective:

Skills:
- Use short, bulleted, action-oriented phrases that communicate your primary and secondary benefits to the prospective employer

• Demonstrate the results you accomplished, and the "Potential Product" you have to offer

• Be specific, using actual figures instead of rounding them off

Employment History:
• In reverse-chronological order, list the companies with which you have worked, the dates of employment and your job titles

Education: Follow the guidelines given above for handling this topic

Special abilities: The same caveats apply here as to the "classic" format. Carefully think about what additional comments to make, as they apply to your objectives.

Look at the forest and the trees.

Other than those shown here, no examples of different resume formats are to be found in Job Search 101. You already have enough information to create a standard resume. Designing one of these will sufficiently serve you. But it may not be in your best interests to have a resume that is just like all the others. If you are going to stand out among your competitors profession- ally, you should use a format that best presents your qualifications, benefits and individuality, not necessarily one that everyone else uses.

Keep in mind a term graphic designers use. It states that "form follows function," meaning that when creating a layout, the objective of the piece should be considered first. The physical form of the layout that will best achieve that goal follows.

This principle can be adapted to mean that you shouldn't create the resume format first and then fit your words neatly into that structure. You should first decide what the major points are that you want to communicate, then plan the format that will best achieve that objective. Keep this in mind particularly when you are using the structures in Exhibits 11 and 12.

Try several layouts, then combine the best parts of each. Could it look better if you turned the page horizontally and presented your information in two columns? What about an audio or video resume? Force yourself to think of new ways to accomplish your goals. Don't start writing any correspondence until you have read Job Search 101 at least once, specifically Chapter Twelve. That chapter alone will help you creatively adapt the final form of your resume and letters to the particular function you want each to perform.

If you don't feel that you can be creative on your own, ask members of your Brain Trust to help you. And ask interviewers to critique your resume and cover letters, particularly if they reject you as a candidate. Perform an autopsy on your correspondence, and try to determine the cause of death. Then create a way to prevent it from occurring again.

Resume "Don'ts":
• Don't force the reader to guess what you are trying to say. Be clear, concise and to the point.

• Don't make unbelievable claims. Be conservative and offer proof to show that you have understated your accomplishments. People know that it takes many people to make success happen, so just show what part you played in a particular event.

- Don't try to hide time that you were unemployed. Always account for your time between jobs. Some people only use the year in their dates of employment to hide time out of work. For example "1988 - 1989" could be two years or two weeks.

- Don't criticize methods or ideas of other people. Show how you creatively improved upon an idea and describe the benefits your company realized from your efforts.

- Don't criticize previous employers or blame your reasons for leaving entirely on them. Rarely is one party at fault, and a mature person will recognize and admit that.

- Don't list negatives, i.e., unwillingness to travel or relocate. Since you obviously have reasons for these restrictions, wait until you are face-to-face with the interviewer so you can explain them.

- Don't make every job or responsibility sound the same as others you've had. If applicable, show that you had ten years of steady growth, not just one year repeated ten times. A prospective employer isn't as interested in someone who has done the same job with different companies as much as she is in someone who has had a variety of experiences. For example, if you are an advertising copywriter, emphasize your experience in industrial writing in one position, radio in another and public relations in another.

- Don't give equal attention to all employment positions. Give greater emphasis to more recent and pertinent jobs.

- Don't crowd the page, making it difficult and uninviting to read. Use "white-space" to make it look uncluttered and provide space for the interviewer to make notes during your interview.

- Don't include your salary history and requirements on your resume. Instead, provide this information either on a separate sheet or in your cover letter. If it is not requested, don't volunteer it until asked to do so.

- Don't list your references on your resume. You may want to state that business and personal references are furnished (not "available") upon request. In any event, be sure to keep a list of their names, addresses and telephone numbers handy for use when you fill out an application. Make sure they know they are being used as a reference.

Once you have finished writing your resume, compare it to the checklist shown in Exhibit 13. Then give it to others to read and critique. This is important because after you write your resume, you will tend to review it to correct the information you have just written. You may lose sight of information that you omitted. When you let others read it, they can evaluate it from the perspective of what is there <u>and</u> what is not there that should be.

EXHIBIT 13: COVER-LETTER/RESUME CHECKLIST

❏ Did you read and re-read each statement to make sure it is concise, action-oriented and credible?

❏ Are all statements complete and current?

❏ Are all statements written to express the benefits you can offer a prospective employer?

❏ Did you proofread all correspondence to check for spelling errors, missing words and proper grammar?

❏ Did you show support for any statements that might at first seem unbelievable? Are your statements convincing?

❏ Did you use short, punchy sentences with action-oriented words? Are all statements clear?

❏ If you decided to state your objective, is it succinct and definite?

❏ Did you remove all irrelevant information that might make the prospective employer stop reading?

❏ Do applicable statements reflect your positive, enthusiastic attitude and create an accurate image of you?

❏ Did you check the list of "Resume Don'ts" to make sure you have avoided them?

❏ Does the overall layout invite the reader to read the correspondence completely?

❏ Did you begin your cover letter with an attention-getting statement, expand on that benefit to stimulate interest, add additional benefits to generate desire, and close with some committing question?

❏ Did you use "bridges" in your cover letter to maintain the reader's interest?

❏ Are your employers and schools listed in reverse-chronological order?

❏ Are there any fingerprints or other marks on your correspondence?

❏ Is the presentation sequence the same for all the sections?

❏ Did you properly use the PREP formula?

❏ Does your resume follow the information in your cover letter, and does it support your career objective?

❏ Does it leave the reader with a feeling that the company will be better off hiring you than one of your competitors?

Printing your resume.

Find a local print shop and have it professionally print your resume. Don't copy it on a Xerox machine. Ask for a recommendation of a good quality paper such as Classic-Laid paper, which creates a high-quality impression. There are also different colors of paper from which to choose, and four Classic-Laid paper colors are particularly appropriate. These include 1) Classic Natural White, 2) Avon Brilliant White, 3) Baronial Ivory or 4) Antique Grey. Don't use a darker color than Antique Grey, or your correspondence will be difficult to read.

Don't reproduce your resume directly from an original printed on a dot matrix printer, which doesn't reproduce well. Have the original typed using a secretarial service with a good quality typewriter, or have it printed with a laser printer.

You should have a few hundred printed. The price will be better at higher volumes, and it may not cost much more to have 300 printed than 200. It will cost you more to have 300 printed in six separate runs of 50 each. If you are planning mass mailings, or attending job fairs and trade shows in the near future, you'd probably want to print 500, depending on your plans. Print enough to meet your needs over the next two months. If you've had no success by then, you may need to change your resume anyway.

Mailing your cover-letter/resume package.

Now you're ready to send your package. When you do, only include your cover letter, resume, and if appropriate your Personal Reply Card (see Exhibit 18). If a salary history is requested, you can send this on a separate form, or include it in your cover letter. Don't send letters of recommendation, references, job descriptions or any other information that will clutter up your package.

Most applicants send their package in a standard, Number 10 business envelope, with two folds in it. These fit nicely in a stack of letters and resumes, each folded piece unobtrusively fitting into the one below it. Your package can stand out among the crowd if you send it flat, unfolded, in a large 9" x 12" envelope.

You could FAX your resume. The positive side of doing so is that yours will probably be the first to arrive, it will be hand delivered to the addressee, and it shows you are interested in the position. It also gives you the opportunity to call to make sure it was received. On the other hand, a FAX may arrive distorted, incomplete or may require an attendant to call and have the FAX re-sent. If you do FAX your resume, write on the cover page that you will be sending a clean copy to arrive in a few days. Then do so. And follow up with a telephone call to make sure it was received in good order.

The option of sending your package by overnight mail will cost between $9.95 (at the U.S. Post Office) and $15.00 (via Federal Express). It presents a good image, is hand-delivered to the addressee, and shows extreme interest. But it could come across as "overkill," and it may be held by a secretary to hand to the addressee (without the accompanying overnight envelope) along with the others when they arrive. It can also become expensive if you do it frequently. But if there is one company for which you really want to work, and you are not sending your package as the result of an ad, overnight delivery can be an effective way to get the reader's attention. Always follow up with a telephone call to make sure your package arrived.

Professional assistance.

One company writes resumes and cover letters for job seekers, and the process is done completely through the mail. You simply contact them to send you an Information Input Package. Once you complete and return the appropriate information to them, they write the resume and send you a draft copy for your comments and approval. When they receive your changes, they finalize the letter and resume and make the copies for you. The company is Marketing Directions, Inc., P. O. Box 715, Avon, CT 06001. The telephone number is 1-800-JOB-HELP.

You may choose other resume services to write your resume. If you do, make sure they keep your individual needs in mind and don't give you a standard resume written for everyone in your job classification.

Audio resumes.

You may choose to send your resume in the format of an audio cassette. If you are seeking a position in telemarketing or as a receptionist, for example, it would be important for the interviewer to hear how you sound. Under these circumstances you could send an audio resume, taped on a cassette.

Don't tape the resume on your home recorder. Go to a studio and have it professionally recorded. Have them make duplicate copies, but leave room at the beginning of the tape so you can individualize each with a specific introduction. You can also leave room at the end for your personalized call to action.

You should present the same information as you would in a written resume but don't just read your resume into the microphone. Write an outline that will prompt you to discuss your job and your benefits and accomplishments. Since most people communicate more formally in writing than they do by voice, your audio resume should sound more like a conversation.

In addition, you can follow these guidelines that advertisers use when writing radio copy:

1) Get attention early in an audio resume. Use the tactics described in the AIDA formula, but adapt them to using sound.

2) Stick to one idea at a time. Discuss only one function at a time for each company. Describe your job and accomplishments; then move on.

3) This is not an interview, so don't plan on taking an hour to present your background. Make your presentation carefully, and don't take more than four minutes to complete your entire "performance."

4) Remember the SALARY acronym (found in Chapter 9), and adjust your speed, accent, loudness, authority, rhythm while using the "you" approach.

5) Write directions on your script to remind you to accent certain words and to slow down to emphasize and articulate certain points.

6) Don't get carried away by using background music and sound effects.

7) Use your name often to register it with the listener. Also include your name, address and telephone number on the label of the tape.

8) Keep a conversational tone, but not too informal. You want to make the listener feel as though you are performing as you would be on the job.

9) Send a cover letter with your audio resume.

Video resumes.

Video presentations may be created in two forms. You could actually have someone interview you, and tape it. Or you could create a video resume and send that to prospective employers. In either case, have it professionally produced.

A video interview would be appropriate if you are seeking a position in a distant city. Have someone actually interview you, using a list of prepared questions, and tape it. Try to keep the time frame down to about 20 minutes. Then send it to the decision maker at your target company, with a cover letter explaining what is on your tape, and how long it will take to view it.

A video resume could be used for careers that require a good physical image. If you want to be a television news or sports commentator, weatherperson or anchorperson, your image will be as important as your skills.

When creating a video presentation, you should adhere to most of the rules that apply to audio resumes. The obvious difference is that you now have the visual dimension to use. Always use a professional company to create your tape and coach you in successful techniques for "performing" your resume or interview. Listed below is a summary of the guidelines to follow:

1) Write an outline for a script and show camera directions on it. Begin with a wide angle shot to let the viewer know the environment. You can close in later for a tighter shot when emphasizing a point. Then open back up to a wider shot to create a more relaxed, conversational atmosphere. Make sure your cameraperson knows when to implement your directions.

2) When creating a video resume, use cue cards to help keep your attention on the camera. You should not read your script, but talk to the viewer, via the camera. Maintain good eye communication. Don't always stare at the camera.

3) Edit the tape carefully. It should be one continuous presentation, without abrupt stops and starts. A professional video company can properly edit your tape, using fades and cuts to dramatize and emphasize your points.

4) Don't exceed a five-minute video resume. Let the viewer know in advance how long the presentation will take by including the viewing time on the label and in your cover letter. You can take more time if you are showing examples of previous air time, speeches or whatever experience you have that is germane to the position.

5) Always send a cover letter with your tape.

6) Don't get carried away with gestures. A video resume gives you an excellent opportunity to use body language effectively, so use it to your advantage. Sit up straight and emphasize points sparingly. Smile regularly and relax. Don't point your finger directly at the viewer, especially during a close-up shot.

Follow-up.

Complete, accurate and timely follow-up is critical to any career search. Keep a list of those people whom you have contacted and pursue them at some future time. Exhibit 14 shows an example of a format for keeping track of the companies and people with whom you have corresponded. You can use this form for both your letter writing campaign and after personal interviews. If, for example, you contacted J. V. Smith at ABC Company on 6/12/91 as a result of an ad, you would write that information on the form. You may have indicated in your cover letter that you would call the person in two weeks; write that date in the column headed First Follow Up. Call J. V. Smith on that date. Depending on the results of that call, write in the date of the next call in the column headed Next Follow Up.

EXHIBIT 14: FORMAT FOR TRACKING CONTACTS

COMPANY NAME	CONTACT'S NAME	INITIAL CONTACT DATE	FIRST FOLLOW UP	RESULTS	NEXT FOLLOW UP
ABC Co.	J. V. Smith	6/12/91	6/26/91		

If you don't feel comfortable following up on the telephone, or if you responded to a post-office box number, you could follow up by mail. On the chart, write the date to send your first follow-up letter. Mail this to arrive about two weeks after you initially sent your package. An example of your first follow-up letter is found in Exhibit 15. It should be a gentle reminder that you haven't heard for them yet, but you are still interested in the position.

EXHIBIT 15: EXAMPLE OF A FIRST FOLLOW-UP LETTER

Dear J. V. Smith:

On June 12, I responded to your ad requesting resumes for the position of Southeast Regional Manager. As of this date I have not heard from you, and I wanted to reiterate my sincere desire to work for ABC Company.

Since responding to the ad, I have done a great deal of research on ABC Company and find it to be a successful organization. Your distributor in Atlanta is particularly impressed with your customer service and product quality.

In case my original resume was mis-directed, I will again summarize my experience. During my last three years in sales, I have demonstrated my

- ability to successfully sell products such as those your company offers and increase territory sales by 42%;

- success in achieving objectives through teamwork;

- competence in creatively building new sales from existing customers to the point that they now comprise 61% of my total business;

- capacity for continued self-education since earning my MBA.

I would like to discuss with you the fit between my background and the opportunity at ABC Company as your Southeast Regional Manager. I am confident that I could make an important contribution to your long-term growth. I am looking forward to hearing from you.

Sincerely,

Write the date to send the second follow-up letter on your tracking form. It should arrive about two weeks hence. Send a letter that is a more firm (but cordial) reminder that you have not heard from them though you are still interested in interviewing for the position. Don't appear too pushy, and don't try to blame them for taking too much time in responding. Just be firm in your desire to be interviewed.

Replying to a rejection response.

At any point in this sequence, you may receive a letter saying that your qualifications have been reviewed, and even though they are impressive the company does not feel they adequately match the requirements for the position. You should follow up such a letter with one similar to that shown in Exhibit 16.

EXHIBIT 16: SAMPLE REJECTION-RESPONSE LETTER

Dear Mr. Smith:

Thank you for sending me your letter stating you chose another candidate for the position of Southeast Regional Manager.

I imagine you rarely receive a thank you note following your rejection letter. But it is just as rare that I receive such professional treatment from a company during my career search. I wanted to let you know that someone acknowledges your professionalism.

I hope your first choice for the position is successful. If another position in your sales department should become available in the future, please keep me in mind. I would be honored to work for a company that handled its applicants in such a considerate manner.

Thank you again for your professional consideration. I am looking forward to hearing from you should another opportunity arise.

Sincerely,

NARROWCASTING

If you limit yourself to responding only to ads in the newspaper, you are exposing yourself to just a small part of all the available positions. And these ads just show the positions that are open now, not those being contemplated for some time in the future.

As the following graph indicates, companies plan for a new position well before they advertise it. Such planning is on-going, done at various times. If you can catch them in this process before they actually place the ad, you can beat your competition to the opportunity. By writing an unsought letter, you can help do this. Send your letter to the person planning the new job (usually a department head and rarely in the Personnel Department) and you can present your skills and benefits without the clutter of your competitors' resumes.

The same principle applies when people leave their jobs. The position will remain open for a certain amount of time before an advertisement is placed for the replacement. Your letter will make them aware of your availability before the ad begins running.

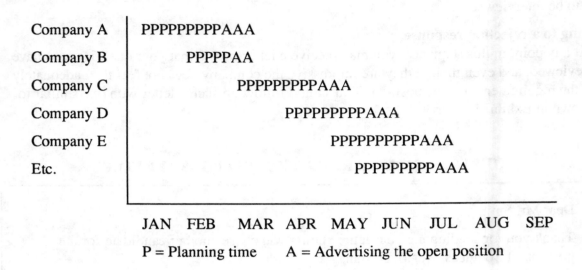

Company A   PPPPPPPPPAAA

Company B   PPPPPAA

Company C   PPPPPPPPPAAA

Company D   PPPPPPPPPAAA

Company E   PPPPPPPPPPAAA

Etc.   PPPPPPPPPAAA

JAN   FEB   MAR   APR   MAY   JUN   JUL   AUG   SEP

P = Planning time   A = Advertising the open position

Before the actual planning process begins, the department manager will usually have the thought in the back of her head that "sooner or later I've got to create a new position to handle that situation." If your letter arrives in that period, you may also move the planning process along more quickly, with you as the only candidate.

Use a rifle, not a shotgun.

One of the most effective ways of creating such opportunities is through a letter-writing campaign. You'll generally hear of this as "broadcasting" your availability. I prefer to call it "narrowcasting" your availability, because broadcasting suggests you are using a "shotgun" instead of a "rifle," or a more carefully qualified approach.

Narrowcasting consists of locating a list of target companies in your industry and then taking the initiative for writing to them. You should first find directories that list companies in your field of interest and then go through them to create your prospect list.

Don't go right to the top.

You could send your narrowcast letters to the president of the target company. It would be logical to assume that if the president read it and forwarded it to the proper party, it would appear as an "endorsement" from the president. It also follows that the recipient of that endorsement would be more likely to contact you if the president had "asked" him to.

However, you'll probably find this ineffective because the president's secretary will most likely intercept your letter and send it to the Personnel Department. Subsequently, most of your responses will be form letters from the personnel department thanking you for sending a letter to the president, but that nothing is available now.

You should also avoid sending your narrowcast letter to the personnel department. They may not even know the opportunities that are in the planning stages and may therefore reject your application on the grounds that nothing is available. And as far as they know, it's true.

You'll have greater success if you address your narrowcast letters to specific department heads. These individuals know exactly how they intend to increase the size of their departments. They may have plans not yet even written or approved but just "on the drawing boards."

A sales manager, for example, may have a plan to increase the size of his sales force by expanding in certain cities. He may want to add a person in the Southeast, but the exact location is yet to be determined. Your letter notifying him of your availability in Atlanta may be just the thing to overcome his inertia and invite you in for an interview.

Writing your narrowcast letter.

Writing an effective narrowcast letter is difficult. You must combine the AIDA formula with other techniques of persuasion. The company's managers may not even know they have a need for a new employee. You have to <u>create</u> that need. Let them know you have the ability to satisfy it and get them to invite you in to discuss the opportunity.

Just as your cover letter began, your narrowcast letter should begin with an attention-getting statement of the benefits you can provide to the company. You must promise a benefit that appeals to the reader's self-interest, which requires that you be as specific as possible. Your "headline" should create immediate, positive impact and lure the reader into the body of the text.

The first paragraph should be short and to the point. In one or two sentences, use the "Five Ws" technique to introduce your point. The Five Ws are Who, What, Where, When, and Why. Look to the first paragraph of the letter in Exhibit 17, which demonstrates this method. It states who you are, what you are writing about, why it is beneficial for the reader to act now, when these benefits should begin occurring and where you are seeking employment.

Customize your approach.

Use some creativity for gaining the reader's attention. If an article has been published that is favorable about the company, include this information in your opening paragraph. Similarly, by reading the "Who's News" section in a newspaper, you may find that a person was just promoted to Vice President for a company in your field. Begin your letter by congratulating him or her on the promotion, then state how you can be of assistance. Let the reader know that you have chosen to apply for employment for some reason other than the fact he was alphabetically listed in the business directory.

Once the reader goes to your next paragraph, you must reward him for doing so by building upon the promised benefit. Expand on your opening paragraph and offer proof that you can do what you claim you can. After you have explained and documented your primary benefit, go on to add applicable secondary benefits.

The **BRIAN** formula will help you organize the remainder of your letter. Start by naming another **B**enefit. It should be related to and continue building your "case." Give a **R**eason why this is important to your current or previous employer. Then make an **I**nference that you can apply the same skills to benefit the reader's company. Use an **A**ffirming question to get the reader to confirm your statements in his own mind. Then go on to the **N**ext benefit. The second and third paragraphs in Exhibit 17 demonstrate the BRIAN formula.

EXHIBIT 17: SAMPLE NARROWCAST LETTER

Mr. Lou Reale
Wayne Industries
Burlington Street
Cincinnati, Ohio 45255

Dear Mr. Reale:

I am an experienced and successful salesman who has increased territory profits by 53% in one year. I seek to apply these skills immediately in a sales position for Wayne Industries in a Cincinnati territory.

Furthermore, by implementing my sales-management skills, I motivated a national sales force to exceed its annual profit goal by 26%. This success entrenched my company in a previously untapped market. I have applied these skills similarly in the past, and I am confident that I can do the same for Wayne Industries. Don't you agree that this would be beneficial?

In addition, I have demonstrated my

- ability to forecast territory sales successfully and accurately,

- personal motivation and determination,

- energetic and competitive attitude,

- confidence in creating innovative and imaginative responses to a variety of selling situations.

I am interested in meeting with you to discuss the possible fit between my background and a present or future opportunity at Wayne Industries. I will call on March 8 to arrange an appointment with you.

Sincerely,

Don't send your resume with this letter. Summarize your benefits and whet their appetite for talking with you. You can expect a large number of rejection responses with this technique. But at least the letters will be written personally and the promise to keep your letter in an active file will be more genuine than with other methods.

Copywriter's techniques.

There are certain techniques that professional copywriters use to improve the persuasive power of their promotional copy. These people are trained to say as much as they can in the least amount of copy, in order to get you to buy their product instead of a competitor's. Perhaps some of these techniques can also help you:

- Descriptions of the reward for using the product are more important than descriptions of the product itself.

- There are two forces at work in your reader's mind. These are skepticism and the desire to believe. Therefore, you do your reader a favor by providing evidence that what you are saying is true.

- Specific statements are more believable than generalities. Don't just say you increased sales a great deal or "almost 50%." Say that you "increased sales by 47%."

- If you want to drive home a point, you have to say it three times. First say that you can "increase sales," then later that you can "exceed objectives" and finally that you can "contribute to improved earnings."

- Make your copy easy to read. Use short words, sentences and paragraphs.

- If you must write a long letter, break up the copy blocks to make it look more inviting to read. Use sub-headlines, keep the opening paragraph to eleven words, use bold type or italics to accent important points, use "bullets," and use leading (additional space) between paragraphs.

- Use "bridges" to start new paragraphs and liberally use the words "you" and "your" when referring to the reader or his company, thus involving him and arousing his interest in your services.

Close the letter with some call to action. Refer back to the information about taking action that was given in the section on writing cover letters. Apply the same techniques with your narrowcast letters. Don't ask the reader to contact you. You should take the initiative to follow up.

The importance of follow-up.

It is critical for you to follow-up after sending a narrowcast letter. Set up a chart as shown in Exhibit 14 to facilitate your follow-up activities. When you follow up, you should use it as an opportunity to send your complete resume or perhaps a testimonial letter. Include some document that will add more fuel to the fire you started with your original letter. You must get the recipient to make some favorable move, preferably to call you for an interview.

If you follow up with the person by letter, use a style similar to that shown in Exhibit 15. Remind him of the letter and briefly summarize your intention and skills. Close with a request for the next step to occur. If you follow up by telephone, ask to speak to the addressee personally.

You may not get through to that person due to travel schedules, meetings or other reasons. Once you reach him, you will get one of three responses. The first is a positive response that creates the opportunity for an interview. The second is a negative response that states there is nothing open now but thank you for your interest. The third is a neutral response that states there are some plans in the offing and that your letter will be held for future consideration.

If you get a positive response, set up a time and date for the interview. If you get a negative response, thank him for his time and send him a rejection response letter similar to that shown in Exhibit 16. But add one more paragraph asking the contact to forward your letter to someone else in the company who might be able to utilize your skills at this time.

If you get a neutral response, immediately ask when it would be a reasonable time for you to wait before getting back in touch with him. It may be a few weeks or months but write the date on your calendar and contact him then.

ADVERTISING YOURSELF.

Imagine a situation in which a person is out of work, doesn't tell anybody about it, then waits at home for someone to call with a job offer. It sounds ludicrous, but this is what happens when a job seeker doesn't use all the means available to him to communicate that he is looking for a job. Placing an advertisement announcing your availability is an often overlooked, yet effective and cost efficient means of doing this. It should not be used in place of your other efforts, but as a valuable adjunct.

A variety of media can promote you in an advertisement. The <u>National Employment Business Weekly</u> regularly has a section called "Talent For Hire," which publishes ads for people seeking positions. Other newspapers offer similar opportunities. You can advertise in the employment, business, real estate, art, travel or sports section of the newspaper, depending on your intended vocation.

Writing an ad about yourself.

Many of the letter-writing techniques you have learned can also be used for writing ads about yourself. Remember to get attention quickly and present your benefits. In a classified ad, with a limited number of words, it is even more important to make every one count.

Don't waste them by starting your ad with "Available" or "Seeking Work" if you are advertising in the Talent For Hire section. The reader knows that you are available because you are advertising in that section of the newspaper. Use action-oriented words that describe your benefits. Generate interest, desire and close with a request to take some kind of action.

You could begin your ad with either of the following two statements. Each of the two has 17 words, so they would cost the same. Which do you think would be more effective?

> Immediately available. Sales person experienced selling industrial products. I will work on commission or salary plus commissions.

VS.

> Sales pro with strong closing skills. Will build profitable territory for industrial products. Commissions or salary plus.

Use your initial words to flag down your prospect. Make some immediate, positive impact and try to draw him into the body copy. Appeal to the reader's self-interest and promise some benefit or reward. Think of your initial words as you would the attention-getting opening statement in your letters.

Write the body copy as engagingly as you would the headline. Always write from the prospective employer's point of view. Provide facts, benefits and enough information so that they will contact you for an interview. Eliminate extra words such as "the." Use short words and statements that are motivating. Use underlines or bold type to accent important information.

Be sure to include the means for the reader to contact you. Just list your address and telephone number. Don't tell the reader to "Call me right away at...." Use advertising as a creative and effective tool, and you will generate additional opportunities. When added to the other weapons at your disposal, your communication strategy will be much more effective.

2) Sales Promotion

Sales promotion is a term that refers to marketing activities (other than advertising, public relations and personal selling) that stimulate the prospective employer to purchase your product more quickly. These techniques typically offer an incentive for the end user to buy your products. You can use similar strategies in your job search.

A) Personal reply card.

You are probably familiar with the postage-paid return card that is included in the direct mail you receive. In the vernacular of the business world, this is called a BRC (business reply card). In your job search, it takes on a different name but its function is the same.

You can create a personal reply card similar to the one shown in Exhibit 18. It can be effective for generating an increased response to your mailings. On one side of the card, create a checklist of positive responses from which the respondent may choose. For example, you could have the recipient check whether she wants you to call for an appointment or send more information or whether she will keep your application on file until an appropriate position becomes available. Make sure you leave room for her to write her name, company name and telephone number.

EXHIBIT 18: PERSONAL REPLY CARD

Front:

> Your Name
> Return Address
> City, State Zip Code

Rear:

❑ Call me to arrange a time
   to meet: ( )_____

❑ Please send me a resume with
   more complete information

❑ We have no positions open,
   but call us in ___ 2 months
   or ___ 4 months to follow up

Name:
Company:
Address:

You have to make arrangements with your local post office in order to implement this idea, create your postage-paid response account and make sure your card complies with their standards. There will be a set-up fee and a cost of about $ .69 per returned card. If you leave a deposit with them, you won't have to pay each time you have your mail delivered. They will tell you when your deposited amount is getting low. Or you can print it as a normal post card and place a stamp on each one.

B) Personal career card.

Most of you have seen business cards and you can adapt them to your career search easily. Create your own personal career card, which is simply a "business" card with your name, home address and telephone number on one side and a brief summary of your skills on the other side. Don't get carried away with the copy on the back of the card. Just list the major skills you have developed, not company names, job titles or dates of employment.

You'll find this card to be useful in many circumstances, particularly at trade shows and job fairs, during informal discussions and interviews, and anywhere you feel you can promote your candidacy for a position. Use it as you would use a business card and give it to everyone possible.

EXHIBIT 19: PERSONAL CAREER CARD

Front:

Rear:

Name Generic Occupation Address, City, State Phone	BS, Marketing, U. of Colorado I have developed skills in: * Planning * Listening * Sales Training * Follow up * Problem Solving * Teamwork * Presentations * Leadership * Time Management * Budgeting

Most local printers will set the type for you. Just write the copy you want to have printed on each side and give it to your printer with instructions to create a standard, two-sided business card. It's a very inexpensive way to set yourself apart from your competition professionally.

C) Advance Card.

All professional people confirm appointments in advance, thus eliminating wasted time on the part of both people involved. An advance card performs this function, as well as serving the dual role of a creative thank-you note if you send it after the interview.

An advance card is a post card with your photo on one half of the back of it. Your local printer can inexpensively produce these for you. Send it to people about a week before your scheduled interview to confirm the time and date of your appointment. Ask the recipient to call you if there is a conflict. Of course, if you don't have a week's time before the interview, you should call the person to confirm.

The advance card is useful if you are meeting someone at an airport or some other public place. If you have not yet met each other, the advance card makes it easier to locate each other as you walk off the plane or search for each other in a hotel lobby.

And finally, your advance card can be easily sent as a quick thank-you note after an interview. It provides an excellent reminder of who you were, especially if the interviewer met with many different people over the course of the day. On the back of the card, next to your picture, summarize the benefits you presented during the interview.

D) Sampling.

Many marketers send consumers samples of their product. The consumer has the chance to evaluate the item without making a purchase. Marketers hope the user will enjoy the product enough to buy it later.

You can apply this same strategy in your job quest. Temporary and volunteer work provide an excellent way for the company to see what you can do and for you to evaluate the company. Refer back to Chapter Three for the information about the benefits and pitfalls of temporary assignments.

E) Literature.

You can create a brief, one page "flyer" to communicate your availability. Simply place it on the bulletin board at your gym, church, the town hall, in office lobbies and anywhere you can get uncluttered, professional exposure. Such a communication device is important if you attend a trade show or job fair. It can be prepared on a home computer, or your printer can make one for you. The example shown in Exhibit 20 serves as a guideline for making your own literature.

3) Publicity

Publicity provides an inexpensive or no-cost means of spreading the word about your availability. The most important benefit of public relations activities is that they add credibility to your cause since the source of the message is usually a disinterested third party.

A) References.

Most application forms will ask you to provide at least three people who may be contacted to substantiate your background and to provide additional information. And most companies will call these people to ask them pertinent questions about you. Your references are important to your success in your search and should be carefully chosen. Make sure you contact them in advance to seek their permission to use their name. Tell them what your goals and recent accomplishments are, and you should remind them of the points you want them to emphasize when a company calls. Use teachers, friends, colleagues, fellow committee members or anyone who knows you well.

When you go to an interview, you may be asked to provide them with both personal and professional references. Keep a list of at least three names in each category (non-relatives), with their addresses, phone numbers and company names.

B) Testimonials.

An unsolicited letter attesting to your skills and performance is worth more than its weight in gold in a career quest. As you begin to collect these, keep them in a safe place, with copies of each to use during an interview.

If you have no unsolicited testimonials, ask your teachers or colleagues to write them for you. Don't fabricate an event, but if you have a legitimate story to tell, have the appropriate person document your efforts and achievements. In this case, make them as results-oriented as you can.

Think of all possible sources of testimonials. Perhaps a teacher once lauded over a paper you wrote, professing to your superior ability to organize and present information. Or maybe a former employer wrote you a letter of thanks after your summer job, inviting you back next year. Whatever the origin, make copies of the letters and keep them ready for use.

C) Published articles.

You may find a local newspaper willing to publish a story about you, if your story contains information that could be helpful to a wide number of their readers. You could write a story about how you volunteered at a local charity during your unemployed time and how you recommend that others do the same. Promote the good efforts of the organization but also communicate your availability in the job market. Write the article with the intention of helping others in your situation, and you may have it published.

D) Support groups.

Churches and other organizations many times create support groups for those who are unemployed. They meet on a regular basis and provide an excellent way to make contacts. When other members become employed, they will remember those who helped them through their time of need and perhaps hire you if the opportunity presents itself. If nothing else, these meetings offer an excellent way to help you maintain a more positive frame of mind. If there is no such group near you, start one.

E) Associations.

Most trade associations, clubs, chambers of commerce, etc. offer membership at little or no charge. These regular meetings provide an excellent way to meet people in the same industry and to promote your candidacy for a position with their firm. They have periodical publications in which you may communicate your availability, often at no charge. These associations offer an excellent opportunity for "networking" and for building relationships with people in your field of interest.

F) The press kit.

Another tool for providing self-marketing information is called a press kit. Companies prepare them to give to members of the press prior to a trade show or other major event. In it are data sheets on the products, general background information on executive personnel, product photographs and testimonials. Most companies formally introduce a new product at a trade show, and the press kit provides the trade newspapers and magazines with the data they need to run feature articles.

You should prepare a press kit for yourself and use it to organize and professionally present your information during interviews. Use your resume to provide your background. Also, keep high quality copies of testimonials and letters of reference in it. If you are seeking a creative position, you should have examples of your work ready to show a prospective employer. You should also include a copy of your college transcript and an extra resume, cover letter and salary history.

Use a good quality folder to keep your information organized. Inside, have samples of all your material ready to use. Prepare about fifty press kits and bring one to every interview. Have each organized so you can easily get a copy of a letter of reference when asked to provide it. A press kit also makes an excellent package to leave with the interviewer after your discussion with him.

PERSONAL COMMUNICATION

Selling

Personal selling refers to promoting your availability on a person-to-person basis. It does not necessarily have to be face-to-face and includes the use of a telephone. It incorporates everything from informal locker-room talks, to networking, cold calls, job fairs, trade shows, telephone calls and interviews. The major benefits of personal communication are that you can use your persuasive skills to handle objections, explain unclear comments, ask and answer questions and ask for some commitment.

Many people dislike the function of selling. The information you will find here recognizes that not everyone is good at selling, wants to or likes to sell. It will show you how to promote your benefits in the most inoffensive yet effective way possible, in keeping with your natural personality.

Personal contact cannot be avoided during your job search. You have to talk with people during interviews and convince them that you are the best candidate for the position. You don't have to manipulate people or try overtly to "sell" them. But you have to make sure all your positive attributes and skills emerge in their best light. Basic skills of personal communication will allow this to occur and reduce the time between job offers.

A) Networking.

It is important to make a large number of people aware that you are out of work. Networking is just the act of calling upon your friends, business associates at former companies, relatives, fellow church members, classmates at school, neighbors, locker-room buddies and anyone with whom you have regular contact. The idea is to let them know that you are available for employment and the type of position in which you are interested.

Don't put them on the spot by asking them for a job or having them ask someone else in their company to give you a job. Your objective is to let as many people as possible know that you are seeking employment and have them spread the word to even more people. Getting a job is as simple as being in the right place at the right time and this is more likely to occur if large numbers of people know you are available.

You'll be pleasantly surprised at how effective this method can be. You can increase awareness of your job search exponentially by having your contacts tell others, who hopefully tell others. But the chances of this announcement going beyond the people you tell it to and those they tell it to are slim. As the direct relationship to you becomes more remote, it becomes less and less likely that people will spread the word. Therefore, you should communicate regularly with your closest group of networking partners. These people have a greater interest in helping you succeed. Don't irritate them with overly frequent contact but keep them abreast of your activities. And thank them later when you secure employment.

Telephone networking.

If you use the telephone to make the initial contacts, let the people know up front what the situation is and ask if they have "a few minutes to talk now," or if it would be better for you to call back later. When making many calls, you should not expect to catch a person at a time that is convenient for him to talk. You'll have to call him back, or you'll have to make arrangements for him to call you back.

Use an answering machine to take your messages at any time during your search. Some people do not feel comfortable using them, but most business people have become used to leaving a message on them. Use the outgoing message as a means of furthering your cause. Don't be cute with your message. Create one that sounds professional and businesslike, not one that will make all your friends chuckle.

Personal networking.

Networking can also be accomplished without using the telephone. If you see people at a party, let them know what is going on in your life. Seek the chance to broadcast your situation whenever you see someone you know. Tell your friends in the locker room, at your child's baseball game, at the local chamber of commerce meeting and during chance meetings at the shopping mall.

Don't overdue networking to the extent that your friends begin to avoid you, and always direct the conversation to another topic when you have accomplished your goal. But remember that being unemployed no longer has a stigma attached to it, and most people will try to help you if they can.

The effectiveness of networking will wane if you have had several jobs in a relatively short period of time. It will be progressively more difficult to call upon your friends every year for search assistance. Abusing your friendship could cost you those relationships in the long run.

This latter point is an important factor about networking. Too often people call upon their friends and business associates only when they need their help in securing employment. Your contacts may feel as if they are being taken advantage of unless you have remained in contact with them during the good times, too. When you seek a person's assistance during a job search, always contact him at its conclusion to let him know what happened and to thank him for his assistance. Also, give these same people a call periodically to let them know you think about them at times other than when you need their help.

Put the shoe on the other foot.

If you have a friend who is unemployed, use reverse networking. Give him or her a telephone call periodically just to see how things are going. Unless you've been "between jobs" at least once, you can't begin to understand the apprehension and stress that occur or how welcome a friend's encouraging voice can be. Few things beat the uplifting feeling that results from a friend's heartfelt call "just to see how things are going" and to find out if there is anything he can do to help.

B) Cold calling.

Calling on people, unannounced, seeking employment is referred to as "cold calling." It can be done in person or over the telephone and it differs from networking in that you are now seeking employment from strangers and from those who have the ability to hire you. If you cold call, you should expect a high degree of rejection. Even with pre-qualified prospects, the chances of finding an opportunity through cold calling are slim.

However, it does provide you with another tool to use in your search. For example, if at 4:00 pm you leave an interview in an office building that is an hour from home, you could call on companies in that building. Rather than waste that hour of prime communicating time driving home, contact companies to find out if they have any opportunities available and, if so, whether they match your criteria.

Ring up your opportunities.

Cold calling by telephone is an efficient way to contact a large number of people in a short period of time. Once you have identified the list of people you want to call, prioritize them in the order in which you feel they should be contacted. If you have generated a list of names from a business directory, keep the directory in front of you as you make the calls. More likely than not, the person you are calling will ask you what you know about the company or why you are calling. The directory will provide the information to answer that question quickly and accurately.

Organize the prospective employers in similar groups. Keep a list of the general benefits you can provide for each segment and possible objections that may come up. Keep a record of what transpired and send a letter to follow up on every call. These letters offer the chance to respond with your resume, a thank-you letter or a letter asking your potential employer to keep you in mind should an appropriate position come up in the future.

Write a script.

You'll find it helpful to use a script when cold calling people on the telephone. All you need is an outline. As you begin calling people, you'll find the conversations will be similar. But if the conversations go off course, a script will get you back on track or give you something to say if there is silence on the other end.

A script will enable you to provide consistency in your presentation and give you the means to duplicate effective techniques. It will also give you the means to reorganize your thoughts after a particularly negative conversation. Most people will be pleasant, understanding and even complimented by your call. But some will not. You have to make the next call as if it was the first one of the day, with a positive expectancy in your voice.

Use a script that is suitable to your conversation style. Most people write more formally than they speak. When you write a script and read from it, you will sound stilted and ill at ease. You'll find it helpful first to write the outline for your script, then record it on a cassette to create a conversational tone. Then make notes from the tape so you'll have something in front of you during your calls. Smile as you speak, and you will sound personable.

When writing the initial outline for your script, use the same techniques and formulas that you used for writing your letters. Begin with an attention-getting opening statement to break the preoccupation barrier. Most people are not sitting by the telephone waiting for you to call them, so your call will probably interrupt their thoughts. You must get them to break away from these other matters with an attention-getting benefit statement. Only then will they devote full attention to you, instead of seeking a way to end the conversation quickly.

Making the initial contact.

As you begin your conversation, it's important to get the listener's attention early. Let the prospect know why you are calling and why it will be in his best interest to listen. State the person's name clearly and frequently, which presupposes that you know the proper pronunciation. If not, call the receptionist first and get the correct pronunciation. Most people like the sound of their name, and it usually gets their attention.

If you expect the call to take long, check for availability to talk, and let the prospect know how long it will take. If the prospect cannot talk now, set a specific time to call back later. Make sure to get agreement on an exact day and time.

C) Job fairs.

Job fairs are comprised of representatives from a wide variety of companies that come together in one location to meet prospective employees. They range in size from those held in a hotel ballroom to a major civic center. They are set up as a trade show with companies organized in separate booths. Here, they offer literature, answer questions about their company and actually hold preliminary interviews.

Job fairs can be effective for personally contacting many people in a short period of time. They are particularly worthwhile for entry-level positions. On the other hand, you may find them impersonal, with a carnival-like atmosphere. But they do add another weapon to your arsenal, so check your newspapers regularly for upcoming fairs.

D) Trade shows.

One way to simulate a job fair and at the same time eliminate your competition is to locate and attend trade shows, i.e., conventions, in your field. A trade show is where many companies offering products and services to a specific industry gather together and set up exhibits to show their wares. These offer an excellent way to contact the decision makers for companies in your specialty directly and uncover information about other companies that you can contact later in your search.

First, contact the show management to obtain a list of the registered exhibitors. Then cross-check the list with your industry directory to find the name of the decision makers for each. Send each a narrowcast letter stating that you intend to be at the show and will be available to interview at that time. Include your hotel address and telephone number and the hours during which you expect to be there.

Once the show begins, you can walk around the exhibits and hand out a descriptive "flyer" about yourself. Don't use a resume at this time, since the person will not have a great deal of time to talk with you. The exhibitor's reason for being there is to contact his customers, so don't interrupt him to talk about your availability. Talk to people when they are not with their customers.

A sample of a summary "flyer" is found in Exhibit 20. Check the show rules to see if you can go into the exhibit hall the evening before the exhibit opens and place your flyer at each booth. Put it in a pre-printed envelope to the attention of the appropriate decision maker.

EXHIBIT 20: TRADE-SHOW HANDOUT

I CAN USE MY CURRENT POLITICAL CONTACTS TO LOBBY SUCCESSFULLY FOR YOUR FIRM IN WASHINGTON.

I am seeking employment as a government-affairs representative in your industry. I have recently graduated from college with a 3.5 grade-point average, and I have four years of experience working for state representatives.

The information below summarizes the skills I have developed.

If you have time this week, I am free to meet with you to discuss a possible opportunity with your company. You can reach me at (telephone number) to arrange a time to meet.

During my career, I have strengthened my skills in the following:

RESEARCHING REPORTS: demonstrated proficiency in acquiring and interpreting data to assist in legislative decision making;

RESULTS: Improved constituent relationships.

ESTABLISHING POLITICAL CONTACTS: worked for the Governor to contact every party representative to communicate his position on several bills;

RESULTS: worked with every Congressperson in the state.

Again, I can meet with you this week. Please call me at (telephone number) so that we may arrange a specific time. I am looking forward to hearing from you.

If you check with the show information people, you may find a list of pre-registered exhibitors, showing the hotel at which they are staying. Call them to follow up on your pre-show mail piece and arrange interviews with them.

Follow up with all the people you contact and send them a note thanking them for taking the time to meet with you. Send a complete resume to them and ask for the next step to occur, i.e., meet for an interview. Call those that seemed to be most interested in talking with you at a later date.

As you can see, there are numerous techniques you can use to promote yourself in the career marketplace professionally and creatively. Communicating your benefits and skills to the largest number of people in the shortest amount of time will greatly reduce the period you will be without employment. If you incorporate these techniques into your career plan, you will creatively, effectively and professionally find the career position of your choice.

ASSIGNMENTS:

5.1   Create a cover letter using the AIDA formula.

5.2   Create a resume using action-oriented benefit statements. Ask others to read it, and make any changes you feel are necessary. Put it down for a day or two while you create other tools. Go back to it and rewrite those parts you now feel need to be changed.

5.3   Create a narrowcast letter using the BRIAN technique.

5.4   Produce your own personal career card and personal reply card.

5.5   Write a first and second follow-up letter.

5.6   Write a letter to send those who reject you as an applicant at this time.

5.7   Create your own personal press kit.

5.8   Make a list of people with whom you feel you can network. Begin calling them.

5.9   Write your telephone cold-calling script.

5.10   Go to the library and find a list of trade shows that are in your field of interest. Plan to attend one that is nearby, and write your letter to arrange interviews with exhibiting companies.

5.11   Create a form to track all the companies to which you have responded or contacted.

CHAPTER SIX

Prospecting For Golden Opportunities

Many people think a job search entails just sending a response to a job opportunity advertised in the classified section in the local Sunday paper. Once the letter is sent on Monday morning, the candidate feels he need only wait for the call from a prospective employer to arrange an interview. Although you will eventually get a call, the classified section has only a limited number of the positions available. To use only this source will limit your opportunities and lengthen the time of your career search.

Most people do not have the time or inclination to wait for an extended period to elapse before getting a job. The best way to reduce the time required to get a job is to contact the largest number of potential employers in the time you have allocated. The key words are potential employers. This presupposes that there is definitely someone out there who is going to hire you.

You could send a letter to every company in the country and eventually get a job. But if you narrow down the list, you'll only contact those with a greater likelihood of hiring you. This is the difference between narrowcasting and broadcasting, minimizing your expenses and maximizing your opportunities.

In so doing, you need to find the names of people to contact who are more likely to hire you than others. The important thing to remember is to find the name of the employment decision maker at a target company as you go through your prospecting steps. Find the name of the manager of the department in which you would be working. Also note the names of other managerial people who could be considered decision "influencers." As you interview with them, they will have input into the decision whether to hire you or not.

As you proceed to contact each person and exhaust each lead, you must replace it with at least one other. And you have to continue performing this process until you start work on your new job. Thus, prospecting is a continuous function and one of the most critical in your search.

Change suspects into prospects.

The function of prospecting actually has three different steps. First, you must establish the criteria for the ideal company and job description for you. Next you must locate names of people and companies to approach (suspects). And finally, you must compare them against the criteria you have established (qualification) and rank them in the order in which you feel they should be contacted, based upon their relative ability to meet your needs. Those who survive this scrutiny make up your prioritized list of people to contact for a job (prospects).

The insert below graphically depicts the elements of this sequence of events. You must constantly seek the names of suspects to qualify against your criteria, whether you are reading the newspaper or looking at packages while walking up and down the aisles in a supermarket. Keep adding more and more companies to your list, qualify them and contact each prospect about a possible employment opportunity.

Step One:	Step Two:	Step Three:
ESTABLISH CRITERIA	**FIND NAMES OF SUSPECTS**	**QUALIFY AND PRIORITIZE**
Description of your ideal employer.	Newspapers Magazines Directories Trade Shows	Assess the ability of each suspect to meet your needs; rank them in the order in which you
Description of your ideal job.	Job Fairs Personal Contacts Schools Personal Observation	will contact them

STEP ONE: ESTABLISH CRITERIA.

Desirable characteristics in a company.

It is easy to find a list of 1000 or more companies to contact in a particular industry. But you have to narrow down this list to the ones that can most effectively meet your needs. Therefore, you must begin by establishing the criteria against which you will evaluate and qualify your opportunities.

Start by creating the list of the characteristics you would like an employer to offer, enumerated in some order of priority. It could include benefits such as medical, dental, and disability insurance. You might add opportunities for a 401K, stock options or a potential equity position. What company personality do you seek, i.e., an aggressive entrepreneurial organization or a solid, blue-chip firm with stability and security? Will you seek a pension plan, or would you rather receive tuition reimbursement? Do you want three weeks of vacation after three years, or would you rather have every Friday afternoon off during the summer months? Should your employer be involved in community or environmental activities, or do these things make no difference to you? And what about child care? Some companies offer this on the premises. Do you want a cafeteria on company property, or would you trade this for a smoke-free environment?

Sample company criteria you might want to evaluate include the following:

Long-term opportunity	Type of supervisor
Promotion from within	How wage increases are determined
Training	Union? Non-union?
Location (near public transportation?)	Financial incentives
	Non-wage incentives
Benefits	Performance appraisal
Counseling	Company philosophy
Car pool	Equal-Opportunity Employer
Large or small	International or domestic
Diversified	Environmentally aware
Modern Facilities	

There are so many individual variables involved with a decision of this magnitude that you must seriously consider making an extensive list of all the options that you seek. Then you should rank these in order of their importance to you. For example, if it's more important to you that a company have international opportunities than a retirement program, the former would be at the top of your list, perhaps as an "A" priority. Those that are not quite as important could be listed as a "B" priority. And those of little consequence could be added to your "C" priority list.

Weigh all the facts; then add your specific criteria to the list of questions found in Exhibit 26 that you could ask a prospective employer. Use these questions to find out the extent to which the company can satisfy your needs. Doing so will make your employment decision easier.

The ideal job description.

Just as you should make a list of employer criteria, you should write a job description for the ideal position for yourself, which will enable you to crystallize your thinking and provide you with a list of additional questions you can ask during the interview.

As you create the description of your "perfect" job based on your career objectives, think about the specific duties and responsibilities that you want to perform. Also, list those that you do not want to perform. Write this description as if you had a magic wand and could create your perfect job.

A good place to find items to add to this list is the Talent-Analysis Sheet you created in Assignment 2.1. Begin by reviewing all the general responsibilities you have had and what you liked and disliked about them. Then review your Self-Analysis Balance Sheet from assignment 2.2. If you felt your strengths were in creativity, planning and writing, and you liked doing these, you would obviously include them in your ideal job description.

List all the specific activities you can think of. Do you want to travel? Will you work overtime if required? Do you want your own corner office and secretary? Do you enjoy making presentations in front of groups, or would you rather not? Should your income be based on salary only, or would you prefer some kind of an incentive compensation plan?

Do you prefer working alone, or do you need close supervision? In either case, make sure you uncover the true management style of your supervisor-to-be. Ask questions about her methods of motivation and reward? And keep in mind that you may or may not be reporting to this person for a long time.

Additional job criteria you might want to evaluate include the following:

Special requirements

Opportunities for continuing education

Initial compensation

Incentives/rewards
Travel requirements/opportunities

Expense policy
People reporting to you

Your own office
Your own secretary

Ability to apply creativity
Physical activities

Overtime
Breaks

Personal freedom
Analytical vs. creative tasks

Contact with upper management
Access to supervisor

Personal challenge
Growth opportunities

If you aren't sure exactly what the title and content would be for your objective, you may want to consider talking with a career counselor to get more information in these areas. For additional information about specific job titles, you could also read a publication of the U.S. Department of Labor called the Dictionary of Occupational Titles.

STEP TWO: FIND NAMES OF SUSPECTS

Having a good idea of the type of company for which you would like to work and the content of the job you want to do will make your search for suspects much easier, since your focus can remain on locating companies that can meet your criteria. And once you list the company names, you can more accurately qualify and prioritize them.

1) Newspapers.

The most obvious place to find suspects that have already been qualified is the classified section of the newspaper. Generally, your local Sunday paper has the largest quantity of companies actively seeking employee candidates, as do the Sunday papers in nearby large cities. But don't ignore local weekly papers for job listings, particularly if you're looking for part-time or entry-level work.

If you are seeking an opportunity in a distant city, you can subscribe to its Sunday paper. If possible, find a local stationary store that sells out-of-town papers and buy one every Sunday. Or if you have friends or relatives living in your target city, you could have them send you the local want ads.

Additionally, The Wall Street Journal publishes The Mart section on Tuesdays, which lists positions at a relatively higher level than many local papers. A sister publication to The Wall Street Journal is The National Employment Business Weekly, which is published every Friday by Dow Jones. In it is a compilation of the current week's help-wanted ads from all of the Journal's regional editions. If you are preparing a national search, it is an excellent source of names. It also contains informative articles to assist in your quest.

The Business section in the Sunday <u>New York Times</u> or the papers from other major cities, such as Boston, Chicago or Los Angeles is another good source of names for positions at all levels in those general regions. While you're in the business section of the <u>New York Times</u> specifically, you should also visit with the last two headings. The first of these is usually the Business Opportunities segment in which you will find information under such topics as "Financing and Business Loans," "Business Connections," "Distributorships/Lines Offered," "Capital To Invest." In addition, there are lists of stores and professional practices for sale, providing an enormous number of ideas for businesses you can start or careers to think about.

The second heading is a separate listing for Franchise Opportunities. Here you will find franchise offerings available for a wide variety of industries, including printing companies, travel agencies, muffler shops, etc. It is a good source of ideas that you might have otherwise overlooked.

Spend the time to do it right.

An effective yet time-consuming way to go through the help-wanted ads entails reviewing the classified section at least three times each Sunday. But if you are serious about prospecting and about your search in general, you have to spend the time to do it correctly.

<u>Step One.</u>

On your first pass through, scan the paper for the job titles that are of immediate appeal to you, and highlight them with a yellow marker. Make sure you read all the small headings and not just the large display ads. For example, if you are looking for a sales position, you could look at the positions listed under "Sales, Regional Manager, Marketing, Management, District Manager, Territory Manager" or any of the other creative names companies have given the sales profession. You should also look under the alphabetical listings for positions in specific industries, such as Insurance, Data Processing, Engineering, etc. for appropriate positions offered in each. As a suggestion, if an ad asks that you call on either of two days, always call on the first of the alternatives.

Some companies have made it difficult for you to review the classified-ad section quickly. In their attempt to be creative, they have caused more confusion and probably a reduced response to their ads. Here are examples of ad headlines from one recent edition of a local Sunday classified section and the position for which the company was advertising:

<u>HEADLINE</u>	<u>POSITION</u>
"We're Stepping into the limelight"	Computer Operator
"Our Diversity is Your Opportunity"	Programmer/Analyst
"We're going places. Want to come along?"	Computer Programmer
"Feel the energy at work"	Reimbursement Analyst

<u>Step Two.</u>

Once you have made your initial pass through the classified section, go back through it again. This time you are looking for companies that are in your field of interest but currently soliciting candidates for positions of no interest to you. Thus you will draw up a list of names and addresses of people to whom you could send a narrowcast letter. Highlight these with a different color marker.

<u>Step Three.</u>

Now you have to go through the section one more time, searching for "hot button" words and ideas for terminology to include in your resume and cover letter. You can find samples of ways to express your background information in terms that are used by the people in the industry itself. Highlight these with yet another color marker. Cut out all the ads you have marked and make a separate pile for each. Then make the appropriate response to each ad, using the new terminology you have found, if it suits your needs and personality. Don't cut out any ads until you have gone through the section as many times as you intend to. Then be careful that by cutting out one, you aren't destroying another pertinent one on the page behind it.

Read all the pertinent sections.

In addition, you can spend more time with the remainder of the papers, reading articles and searching for names of people to contact. Read the papers with a broad-tip marker in hand. Every time you see information about a company in your field of interest, highlight it and cut it out. Then send a copy of the article with a letter to that person, making some favorable comment about it. Every article about people who were just promoted or changed jobs presents an opportunity for two letters. First, you can write to congratulate them and offer your services to help them in their new position. Secondly, you can write to fill the position they just left.

As time permits, go through the other sections that are of particular interest to you and cut out the ads. If you want to go into the travel or real-estate industry, for example, the ads in those sections will provide the names of other prospects to whom you can send your narrowcast letter.

If you are really committed to your career search, you can expect to spend many hours with newspapers, even though only a small percentage of opportunities are listed in the want ads. This will give you an idea of the total number of hours per week you can expect to spend in your search overall.

It's important to look for suspects in a variety of places. Your competitors will be searching for names in the newspapers, too. So you can minimize your competition by finding names where others are not looking.

2) Magazines.

Another source of suspects is the magazines associated with almost any industry or interest. These can be directly related to your **business interests** (<u>Purchasing News, Architect, Management Review</u>), or **general interest** (<u>Sailing, Tennis, Golf Digest</u>, etc.), or even **weeklies** (<u>Time, Newsweek and Business Week</u>). A list of trade journals in your field of interest can be found in the <u>Standard Rate and Data Business Publications Directory</u>, 5201 Old Orchard Road, Skokie, IL 60076. Another useful source is <u>The Standard Periodical Directory</u>, Oxbridge Publishing Company, Inc., 40 East 34th Street, New York, New York, 10016.

Go through the journals and read the articles and ads. Among other things, you will find names of people to whom you can send your narrowcast letter and information about companies and their product lines. The authors of the articles themselves can be targets for you. Send them a copy of their article along with a cover letter discussing it. And don't forget that many industry journals also have employment opportunities listed in them.

3) Directories.

Just as there are trade journals for almost every vocation and avocation, there are directories for them. Your library is an excellent source of directories. The chamber of commerce for your target city also has directories available for a nominal fee (usually $20 to $50). A source of directories for hundreds of different topics can be found in <u>The Guide to American Directories,</u> B. Kline and Company, 11 Third Street, Rye, New York, 10580.

Business and professional associations offer directories of their members. <u>The Directory of Connecticut Manufacturers,</u> for example, is published annually by the Connecticut Business and Industry Association and provides details on its members in a variety of ways. It lists them alphabetically, geographically and also under product headings. Each listing gives the company name, address and telephone number, officer's names, SIC Code, the number of employees, approximate gross sales and a description of their product line. For less than $100, this or similar directories provide an excellent source of suspects and information you can use to qualify them.

For additional information, look into the <u>Encyclopedia of Business Information Sources,</u> Gale Research, Book Tower, Detroit, MI 48226. You should also go to your library for a copy of the <u>Encyclopedia of Associations</u> for more listings.

Industry associations also publish lists of company names. For instance, the <u>Medical Device Register</u> lists almost every healthcare manufacturer permitted to sell in the United States. It contains over 10,000 supplier listings, with each company's full name, address and telephone number, method of distribution, number of employees, sales volume by product line, and officers' names. The <u>Medical Device Register</u> is available by writing Medical Device Register, 655 Washington Blvd., Stamford, CT. 06901, or by calling 1-800-222-3045.

For a wide variety of financial data, you could look to the <u>Dun and Bradstreet</u> or <u>Standard and Poor's</u> directories. The <u>Thomas Register of American Manufacturers</u> offers more information about the company's sales and product line.

Don't overlook the obvious.

One regularly overlooked directory is the Yellow Pages. This displays company names under many different headings. It lists addresses and telephone numbers, and the display ads provide even more product information. When you travel to other cities and stay in hotel rooms, don't forget to review the Yellow Pages there. Write down the information, or have the local telephone company send you a copy of their Yellow Pages directory.

4) Trade shows.

If you know exactly the industry in which you want to work, you can pursue suspects via a trade show. Most industries have one or more shows, and these are held nationally, regionally, locally, monthly and annually. They may be in convention centers, civic centers or hotel ballrooms, and they present a qualified source of information for you.

The directory for each trade show provides you with a list of companies, addresses and product descriptions. Most have the booth numbers and a map of the exhibit layout to assist you in planning your routing among the exhibits. The show program lists the speakers and seminars available, which again poses a list of suspects for you.

5) Job fairs.

Closely associated with trade shows are job fairs. These are made up of potential employers who assemble in one place to interview with potential employees. These provide excellent opportunities to contact personally a large number of people in a short period of time.

6) Personal contacts.

Personal contacts offer a significant means of generating names of suspects and at the same time information with which you can qualify them. Just think about everyone you could contact: friends, previous employers, teachers, colleagues, business associates, employees at the local chamber of commerce, alumni, fraternity/sorority brothers and sisters, the receptionist at the target companies, customers, suppliers and competitors of target companies, networking clubs, support groups, your church, PTA, athletic club, etc., etc.

Every chance you get, ask people for referrals or names of people you can contact about a possible position. Don't just ask your contacts a vague or general question. If you say, "Do you know of anybody looking for an employee with my skills and objectives?," they may not immediately think of anyone. Be specific in providing them with a smaller frame of reference from which to choose and a name may "pop" into their mind.

For example, you may be on an interview and the interviewer (or you) decides that the fit between you and the position is not right. Ask him if he knows whether any of his suppliers are looking for employees. How about their customers? Other departments or divisions in the same company? The more you can limit their frame of reference in answering each question, the more likely they will be to think of opportunities which they might have otherwise overlooked.

7) Schools.

An excellent source of entry-level positions can be located through the vocational guidance counselor at your high school or college. Many colleges offer lifetime assistance for their graduates, and the alumni associations may offer similar services.

Contact the Career Placement Director at your alma mater and find out what opportunities they have for experienced candidates. Ask them what companies in general are hiring in your specialty. And while you're there, ask them to critique your resume and cover letter.

8) Personal observation.

As you can see, there are many sources of suspect's names, some more obvious than others. In order for you to locate them, you must be continuously on the lookout for new opportunities. A suspect could be the name of a company on the side of a truck, a billboard or even a label for a can of hair spray in the supermarket. Every business card, magazine, bumper sticker, newspaper, sweat shirt, etc. could provide the name of a potential prospect for you. You can uncover more names of suspects on restaurant place mats, union hiring halls, signs on buildings, car cards in subways, and on directories in the lobbies of office buildings.

What to look for.

As you are looking for names of people to contact, record information that will later help you qualify your prospects. Find out about the company's history, annual sales, management philosophy, product line and anything else that will help you compare and rank the target companies against the criteria you have established. As you begin to weed out those who cannot satisfy your needs, you'll have more time to apply your energy to contacting those who do meet your needs.

STEP THREE: QUALIFY AND PRIORITIZE

Now you have a list of your criteria and a list of potential companies to contact. The last step in this sequence requires only that you compare the two lists and eliminate those potential employers that do not meet your employment criteria. Once you have a final list of prospective targets, all you need to do is to decide the order in which you will approach them and how much time you will allocate to each.

If a company has an immediate need for someone with your skills, is actively seeking that person, and meets the bulk of your criteria, you would rate it as an "A" prospect. If it offers an opportunity that could be developed in the short term, and it meets more than half (or whatever limit you set) of your criteria, you could rate it as a "B" prospect. If the opportunity will take a relatively long time to develop, and/or they don't even meet half of your criteria, you could label the company a "C" prospect and approach it later.

Constantly reevaluate the individual priority designation since it could change at any time. Through a promotion, acquisition or other unforeseen event, a "C" prospect could jump to an "A" prospect quickly, and vice versa.

Start your search by first contacting all the "A" priority companies either by mail, telephone or a personal visit. Once you have exhausted this list, you can begin corresponding with the "B" targets, and then the "C" prospects. It is unlikely that you will exhaust one category before moving on to the next. You'll find that you will do everything you can on the "A" prospects, and while you are waiting for responses or interviews, you can work on the "B" and "C" targets. Of course, while doing all this, you are looking for new suspects to keep filling the pipeline.

ASSIGNMENTS:

6.1 List all the characteristics you would prefer your employer to have. Rank these in order from the most to the least important to you.

6.2 Write a description of the perfect career position for you.

6.3 Begin pursuing names of people and companies to contact, and assess these against the criteria you established in assignments 6.1 and 6.2. Create a list of target companies, then prioritize and contact them.

CHAPTER SEVEN

Creating Your Job-Search Plan

Strategic planning is necessary in order to place all your activities in their proper sequence. It allows each element to operate synergistically with the others, not in opposition to them. And it provides the framework which directs all your actions toward the accomplishment of your objective.

Planning your job search is a <u>process</u>, not an end unto itself. You must create a document that is goal-oriented, operational, flexible and current. It becomes and remains this way through regular evaluation and revision. Completing your job-search plan will force you to think about where you are now, where you want to go and how you can get there. And the resulting plan will unfold as you create ways to realize your long-term objective.

Your Mission Statement.

Your plan maintains its focus on your <u>objective</u> through the Mission Statement, which in this case is a statement of the long-term vision of what you want to become "when you grow up." Every plan should begin with one. It is a verbalization of the results you expect from your career search, and you should memorize it so you can recite it to yourself every day. It will motivate you and direct your attention.

It will also serve as your Objective statement on your resume, should you decide to include it. Generally, your mission statement will remain intact over the course of your career, but your short-term goals will change as you reach plateaus in your life.

Your marketing objectives.

As you keep a long-range focus on your ultimate mission, your interim objectives serve as the checkpoints against which you can evaluate your relative progress. You should consider several important features about these objectives. In order to be operable, they should be specific, time-oriented, measurable and motivating. And of course, they should be written, which is the intention of your ultimate plan.

1) Specific.

At what do you aim when you throw darts at the dart board, shoot a basketball or park your car? You obviously aim at the bull's eye, the hoop or the space between the other cars. Your career objective provides the same sort of target for your job search. In order to focus your activities on achieving your objective, the goal itself must be to create a specific target at which to aim.

If you set an objective of "getting a job," you can achieve your objective easily. At some point in your life, you'll probably get a job. You may not be doing what you want to do, where you want to do it and at the price you feel it's worth, but it will be a job. And that's all you set out to accomplish.

On the other hand, you could say you want a position as a computer programmer for a major oil company in Houston, Texas, beginning at $X0,000 per year. Now you are directing your thoughts and actions toward the achievement of something you want. You know exactly what it is that you are seeking, where it will take place and the price at which you will accept it. Now your activities can be better directed toward reaching your goal.

2) Time-oriented.

You could have your specific objective in mind but still procrastinate in performing the actions required to achieve it. Therefore, you should set a date for its attainment. By setting an ultimate date, you can then work backwards to create interim deadlines. The attainment of each of these will keep your search on course and on schedule.

If you graduate in May, you'll probably want to have a job by then. So in September you could begin writing your plan to accomplish that fact. Your objective could read, "By 5/1/9X, I will have a position as a computer programmer for a major oil company in Houston, Texas, beginning at $X0,000 per year." Now you have an objective that provides a prospect list (the oil companies in Houston, Texas), a geographic location, a target salary and the date by which you will have it.

3) Measurable.

Because your objective is now specific and time-oriented, you can regularly assess your progress toward its attainment. If you set interim goals, you'll be in a much better position to do this assessment and make the necessary corrections in your actions.

For example, you could decide that by your winter break, you will have already sent letters to the oil companies in Houston and probably arranged interviews with them. By your spring break, you could plan to be on your second or third interview, with a job offer expected shortly.

If by your winter break you have not started contacting the oil companies, you need to begin doing so immediately. In order to reach your goal, you must <u>commit</u> to achieving it. An objective is merely a group of words, unless you dedicate yourself to making it happen. If an interim checkpoint comes and passes, and you have not achieved it, you need to re-assess your position immediately and recommit to getting it done.

4) Motivating.

If you have set your goal so high that it cannot be attained, you're setting yourself up for failure. A recent college graduate's goal of becoming president of a Fortune 500 company with an annual income of $3,000,000 is lofty, specific and measurable, but it is unlikely to be attained shortly after graduation. You could set that goal as your mission statement, then set interim, shorter-range goals to lead to its accomplishment. As you perform each activity and reach each plateau, you experience feelings of success that will sustain your energy and maintain your focus on your long-term mission statement.

Killing time is suicide.

Time management is a critical part of your job-search action plan. You must organize your activities on a regular basis and in the proper sequence. Then you have to utilize your limited time to implement all the actions.

A good starting point is to organize the attainment of your ultimate objective into interim plans, each with its own short-term goals. For example, during the first month of your quest, you should decide to write your resume, cover letter and narrowcast letter. And you'll also want to get a copy of all pertinent directories and go through those to establish your list of "A," "B" and "C" priority prospects.

Create monthly, weekly and daily plans.

An example of how to organize these activities is presented in Exhibit 21. Begin by organizing your time on a monthly basis. On each day, list actions that could be performed and the approximate sequence in which they should be done. As you can see, there is not a great deal of free time available during the initial stages of your search.

EXHIBIT 21: SAMPLE MONTHLY PLAN

SUN	MON	TUE	WED	THU	FRI	SAT
					1 Create monthly plan NEBW Write resume	**2** Talent-Analysis Sheet Write cover letter
3 Review Sunday papers Self-Analysis Balance Sheet	**4** Finalize resume Price/Place decisions Daily Plan	**5** Networking calls WSJournal Press kit Daily plan	**6** Career Card Follow up letter Daily plan	**7** Temp Letter Library Daily plan	**8** Prospecting NEBW Advance Card Daily plan	**9** Check wardrobe Create Brain Trust Price Formula Join gym
10 Review Sunday papers Write weekly plan	**11** Daily plan Networking	**12** Daily plan Prospecting WSJ Networking	**13** Daily plan Job Fair Networking	**14** Daily plan Practice questions Prospecting	**15** Daily plan NEBW Prospecting	**16** Create presentations Post-interview checklist
17 Write weekly plan Review Sunday papers	**18** Daily plan 10:00 Interview A/V aids	**19** Daily plan Prospecting Practice questions WSJ	**20** Daily plan Prospecting Trade show READY formula	**21** Daily plan Closing techniques	**22** Daily plan NEBW SALARY AIDA	**23** Rejection-response letter
24 Write weekly plan Review Sunday papers	**25** Daily plan 1:00 Interview	**26** Daily plan WSJ	**27** Daily plan Networking calls	**28** Daily plan Prospecting	**29** Daily plan NEBW Progress Checklist	**30** Evaluation

You must get as much information communicated early in your quest as possible. The more people you contact, the more quickly your "network" will grow. It can take many weeks to get the wheels turning at full speed, and the earlier you begin, the less time your search will take.

Create your weekly plan.

Next, you need to segment your monthly plan into a more detailed, manageable weekly plan. Every Sunday evening, take an hour or so and plan your upcoming week. Exhibit 22 shows an example of a form you can use to do this. You can combine your weekly and daily planning activities. Take six copies of the form in Exhibit 22, and write each day of the week at the top of a different page. On each, list all the activities from your monthly calendar for that day. List all the phone calls you need to make and the letters to send. Leave room to write in all the events that will come up as the week unfolds. As you prepare your week, try to plan activities during the working day that require contact with people in their offices. Plan to do your direct-mail work and review of directories in the evenings and on the weekends.

EXHIBIT 22: SAMPLE DAILY PLAN

Things to do today: November 4

DO	CALL		
A Priority	**Person**	**Number**	**Objective**
1. Finalize my resume/cover letter	1. College Placement Office		
2. Work on my Talent-Analysis Sheet	2. Creditors - tell them of situation		
3. Finish my Self-Analysis Balance Sheet	3. Unemployment office		
4. Select paper color for my resume	4. Networking contacts		
5. Write my telephone cold-calling script	5. Brain-Trust Members		
6. Investigate potential employment agencies	6.		
7. Make a list of networking contacts	7.		
8.	8.		
9.	9.		

B Priority	**Follow up necessary:**
1. List of 20 good points of present situation	Call ads in Sunday paper
2. Investigate geographical locations	
3. Write daily credo	
4.	
5.	
6.	**Expenses:**
7.	27 miles
8.	Chamber of Commerce Directory ($25)
9.	

C Priority	**Appointments:**
1. Create a tracking form	**Time Person Place**
2.	
3.	
4.	

To do this evening:	**To do this weekend:**
Add to plans for remainder of the week	Review my wardrobe - make changes
	Join a gym
	Call people to form my Brain Trust
	Complete my pricing formula
	Visit library for directories

Get in the habit of reviewing and updating your plans so you focus your attention on what else you could be doing to achieve career success. Ask yourself: "What else can I do right now to achieve my goals?" and "What is the most effective use of my time right now for securing a position?" Before you do anything, ask yourself: "Will this activity bring me any closer to the achievement of my objective?" If so, do it. If not, don't do it, but look for some activity that will.

Planning tips.

1) Allocating time.

Always allow more time than you expect an event to take. And keep a list of "filler" tasks handy that you can perform during any unexpected free time. These could be "B" or "C" projects or just minor telephone calls you have to make.

Generally speaking, events will take more time than you initially allocated. For instance, as you begin interviewing, a one-hour appointment could easily take an extra hour. Allow flexibility in your schedule to accommodate unforeseen or time-consuming events, and always have your "filler" tasks ready to perform as unplanned time becomes available.

2) Don't over-correct.

Don't feel that you have to review every detail of your plan every day. Doing so will lead to over-correcting it, especially early in your career search when you are not experiencing a great deal of success from all your intense activities. As you begin to implement your plan, look for things that are no longer necessary. Look for tactics that you haven't used for a while and see if now is the time to utilize them to get you back on track. Look at your plan periodically just to make sure you are doing everything you wanted to do and those things are achieving the results you wanted.

3) Take time to do it now.

All this work that you do early in your search will lay the groundwork for future accomplishment. If you take the time to create a persuasive, professional resume and cover letter, your total search time could be enormously shortened. A six-hour investment in time now may reduce your term of unemployment by weeks or months. The time spent to plan your activities, set your price and choose your location may benefit you with years of happiness in a fruitful, rewarding career.

YOU'VE ALREADY WRITTEN YOUR JOB-SEARCH PLAN.

If you've taken the time to complete the assignments at the end of every chapter, your efforts will pay off here. Each of these will compose a section of the plan you are about to organize. In essence, you've already completed the contents of your plan, and all that remains is to write it.

Major headings.

Mission statement. Your career plan will be organized under several headings. Begin it with the sentence (Mission Statement) you wrote in assignment 2.8.

Personnel Plan. This is a list of the people in your Brain Trust whom you can count on to offer advice, assistance and emotional support. It may be found in your response to assignment 2.5.

<u>Financial Plan</u>. Outline your income and expense situation, which is composed of the information you assembled in assignment 4.1.

<u>Marketing plan</u>. Your marketing plan organizes all the data you assembled about your product, place, price and promotion and the ways in which you can implement them to achieve your objectives.

> <u>Marketing Objectives</u>. Objectives come first and serve as the motivating force throughout your career search. Begin with a statement of your specific, time-oriented, measurable and motivating objective. You must have that goal fixed in your mind so that you are always thinking and performing in terms of your goal.

> <u>Marketing Strategies</u>. This section creates the overall direction and emphasis of your actions. Each statement should outline the general focus of your product, place, price or promotion activities. Each should explain how the specific tactics will be implemented for that category, in order to achieve the final objective.

> <u>Marketing Tactics</u>. The real meat of your plan lies here. List the specific tasks you will perform, on a day-to-day basis, to achieve your objectives. The proper implementation of these will result in a job offer.

Once you combine all the assignments with a list of specific tactics, your job-search plan will resemble that shown in Exhibit 23. The numbers in parentheses indicate the assignments you have already done to compile this information. Simply fill in these blanks, and you will have a complete job-search plan.

EXHIBIT 23: YOUR JOB-SEARCH PLAN

1. Mission Statement (2.8)

2. Personnel Plan (2.5)

3. Financial Plan (4.1)

4. Marketing Plan

>   4.1 Objective

>>   4.1.1   By X/X/9X (2.6) I will have secured my career position (2.8) with an annual income of $(4.2), in the city of (3.2).

>   4.2 Strategies

>>   4.2.1   I will strengthen all the characteristics that need developing in order to offer the most professional and ideal product at the highest possible price.

>>   4.2.2   I will implement both mass and personal communications programs to maximize the quality and quantity of professional contacts.

>>   4.2.3   I will organize an effective and continuous search to uncover the names of people and companies that I will qualify to create a prioritized list of prospects.

4.3 Tactics

4.3.1   What can I do to strengthen my weak areas (2.3)?

4.3.2   In what career position would my strengths be best suited (2.8)?

4.3.3   What can I do to continue my education?

4.3.4   How can I continue (or begin) a physical-conditioning program?

4.3.5   What can I do to improve my physical appearance (clothes, weight, hair cut, shoeshine)?

4.3.6   What can I do to improve and/or maintain my self-confidence?

4.3.7   In what ways can I capitalize on the positive aspects of my present situation (2.7)?

4.3.8   What can I do to solicit the help of those in my Brain Trust (2.5)? Who else could be added?

4.3.9   Is there anything I can do to improve my present employment situation so I don't have to make a career change?

4.3.10 How can I demonstrate the benefits I have to offer an employer?

4.3.11 What can I do to improve the skills I bring to the market (2.9)?

4.3.12 Have I adequately investigated all the geographical options available? What else could I do (3.1)?

4.3.13 In what newspapers and magazines will I place an ad for myself?

4.3.14 How can I make my promotional efforts more creative, credible, complete, current, convincing, concise and clear?

4.3.15 Who could objectively critique my resume and help me re-write it (2.5)?

4.3.16 Did I review my resume against the checklist (Exhibit 13)?

4.3.17 In what other ways can I generate attention, interest, desire and action in my correspondence?

4.3.18 What other questions could I ask an interviewer in order to uncover more information about the position?

4.3.19 How could I better respond to questions during the interview?

4.3.20 What else could I do to evaluate my results and change my plans accordingly ?

4.3.21 Who else can I call upon to implement a networking campaign effectively?

4.3.22 What other closing techniques could I use to gain more commitment and job offers?

4.3.23 What can I do to improve my voice using the SALARY technique?

4.3.24 How can I improve upon my first and second follow-up letters and also my rejection-response letters ?

4.3.25 What else can I add to my personal press kit ?

4.3.26 What sources of uncovering names of suspects could I use that I am not presently using?

4.3.27 Could I use other organizational patterns to improve my presentations?

4.3.28 What objections come up regularly, and how could I handle them more successfully?

4.3.29 How could I make my employment agent more effective?

4.3.30 What other techniques could I use to improve my time management skills?

What you say is as important as how you say it.

If your tactics are going to be most successful, you must write them in a way that will be most stimulating. The tactics described here are offered as questions for this reason. They should stimulate your thinking and at the same time create a system to help you find new ways to implement your actions.

Questions will provoke creative thinking to a greater extent than will a statement. Statements seem to have a "finality" about them. They tend to make you think that you now have all you need to know about the subject. On the other hand, questions give a feeling of "beginning." They indicate that more thought must be applied and additional alternatives sought before the final decision surfaces.

Applying the Rule of Twenty Answers.

The plan above offers a systematic way for you to ask and answer questions. Thirty tactics are listed. Every day, you will focus on one tactic and devise twenty ways to implement it. In your Career Journal, sequentially number the next thirty blank pages 1 through 30. At the top of each, write down one of the questions you have created for your tactics. Along the left-hand side of the page, from top to bottom, write the numbers 1 through 20, each on a different line. Every day, pick a new tactic and write twenty answers to that question.

For example, the person who devised the plan in Exhibit 23 would write, at the top of page 1: "What can I do to strengthen (**weak area**)?" Then he or she would list twenty things to do that would help strengthen and develop that characteristic. On day two, our planner would write at the top of page 2: "In what career position would my strengths be best suited?" Twenty answers would then be listed. Of course, you can list more than 30 tactics and each day continue asking more questions of yourself.

Aim for success, not just activity.

As you create your list of answers, make sure you do it to produce results rather than activities. For example, you could have a goal of making ten prospecting calls on the telephone every day. This is specific and measurable, but it is not success-oriented. You could make ten calls and never talk with one employment decision maker. Set success goals. Re-state your tactics with results in mind. Say "Every day I will begin telephone prospecting and continue until I have made five appointments for interviews."

As you go through this process you'll come to realize there are really only four elements in successful career planning. First you have to have the **right people**. They include yourself and the benefits you have created, and equally important, the Brain Trust of close associates you have assembled.

Second, you have to use the **right process**. You must create an organized, sequential plan based on rational thinking and specific, measurable objectives.

Third, you must have the **right implementation** of your plan. You must have the discipline to work from your strategic plan, implementing your tactics effectively and efficiently. And you must regularly review your relative success.

Finally, you should have the **right expectations**. The objectives must be important to you. They will have no motivating effect if you are striving for goals that are not what you really want. Therefore, your objectives must also be attainable, and you must be committed to achieving them.

ASSIGNMENTS:

7.1 Create a format for a monthly and daily plan that you feel comfortable using.

7.2 Using the outline in Exhibit 23, complete sections 4.1 and 4.2. Write this plan in your Career Journal.

7.3 Make a list of 30 tactics you could implement in your job search, similar to those in Section 4.3. At the top of each of the next 30 pages of your Career Journal, write one of the tactics you listed. Down the left hand side of the page, write the numbers 1 - 20, with space between each. Every morning, take a different page and create 20 ways in which you can address the question it poses.

7.4 Each day, add to your monthly plans each of the 20 items you listed in Assignment 7.3.

CHAPTER EIGHT

The Early Stages Of The Interview Process

Every interview tends to take on its own personality. As you are led down the hallway and turn the corner into the interviewer's office, you can feel the tension mount. If you have any desire at all for the job, you will feel concurrent feelings of positive anticipation and anxiety.

During these critical first few seconds, it's important that you project an aura of confidence and self-control. You will perform most successfully at this time if you understand what is about to happen and if you have carefully prepared for it.

Practice perfectly.

Preparation for an interview takes several forms. You must, of course, be thoroughly knowledgeable about your product's benefits and the needs of the company to which you are trying to sell them. In addition, you must be aware of and practice the skills involved with successful interviewing. These include presenting your benefits, asking and answering questions, handling objections and asking for the job.

As others have said, practice doesn't make perfect. Practice makes permanent. Only perfect practice makes perfect. Therefore, you have to perfectly practice making presentations, answering and asking questions, handling objections and asking for the job. Until you can do all these "with your eyes closed," you will not be at your peak performance level during the interview.

The interview grading system.

You can look at the interview process as a grading system. If there are 100 possible things you can do correctly or incorrectly during the interview, each is worth 1 point. If your shoes are not shined, if you arrive late, if you don't offer a firm handshake and if you slouch in your chair, you've lost four points before you even begin speaking. Every detail is important. You may need a "90" or higher just to be asked to return for a second interview and a "95" or more if you can expect to get the job offer.

The process becomes more confusing when you consider that each interviewer has his own grading system. Furthermore, not all interviews are conducted in the same manner and the same individual may conduct each interview with you in a different way at different times. Yet even with all these variables, you will be more successful if you properly prepare and practice for every interview. The more you do this, the less time your job search will take.

Types of interviews.

Even though individuals will conduct interviews differently, there are four basic types of interviews. You'll find that most situations will include a combination of the four, and they will differ in their application and content.

1) The structured interview.

The first type is relatively structured, and it follows a previously prepared format or script. But you are less likely to experience this situation than one in which the interviewer has a prepared list of questions. The benefit to this process is that every candidate is asked to respond to the same questions, and the answers to each are written down for review later. The interview may actually be recorded, and the tape could be sent to the home office for evaluation in lieu of sending you there for an interview.

2) The typical interview.

The second type is less structured and more typical. In it, the interviewer asks specific questions that are directly related to the job requirements and your ability to fulfill them. She will ask questions as a prompt to seek clarification or more information. You'll find most interviews follow this format, and they are usually emotionally uneventful, particularly after the butterflies in your stomach stop flying.

3) The stress interview.

There is another situation commonly referred to as the stress interview. In it, the questions are asked in rapid fire order by interviewers that appear to be unfriendly. It is unlikely you will ever be subjected to this type. The only justification for its use is to determine how well you perform under pressure.

4) The unstructured interview.

The final major interviewing pattern is more free-flowing. In this, the interviewer tries not to influence your remarks and allows maximum freedom in the response. You will hear questions similar to "Tell me about yourself" or "Please tell me more about why you ...." And you will also hear many one-word questions such as "Why?"

Atypical interview situations.

The above situations could occur under a variety of circumstances, such as in a hotel room, a restaurant, an airplane or in the exhibitor's lounge at a trade show. Not every interview is the typical one-on-one meeting in the interviewer's office, and you'll perform better if you are prepared for any eventuality.

1) Group interview.

This is a presentation to many people at the same time. It includes situations where from two to thirty people are "interviewed" at the same time. They are usually general in format and allow little if any opportunity for questions. The company representative will provide an overall description about the company and the position and ask that those who are interested remain to interview on a more personal basis.

2) Multiple interviewers.

You may also find yourself in a situation with two or more interviewers. This could be a "training" interview where the interviewer is showing a trainee how to ask and answer questions. Or it could be a situation where two people are interviewing as a team in order to hasten the process.

If you find yourself being interviewed by two or more people at the same time, there is a helpful way to remember their names. Ask for their business cards and arrange them in front of you as you would a seating chart. This will enable you to recall their names correctly and frequently refer to them by name. It will also remind you to send each a thank you note after the interview.

3) Telephone interviews.

Telephone interviews represent a special challenge. The caller will most likely catch you at a time when you are not prepared. Ask if you can call the person back or have them call you back at an appointed time if he catches you off guard. It's better to be in a quiet place, surrounded by your notes than it is to discuss everything on an impromptu basis.

Remember to control your voice qualities by using the SALARY technique found in Chapter Nine. Take notes and remember to smile as you speak. Try to eliminate any distractions and if necessary have your spouse attend to your children while you are on the phone. Devote your total attention to listening and attempt to "hear" the interviewer's vocal changes that indicate either a positive or negative reception to your comments.

4) Travelling overnight to an interview.

Flying or driving a great distance for an interview is not really difficult, but it can create greater apprehension than other interviews because you are less familiar with the surroundings. For some people the stress of flying alone causes anguish. But there are a few simple measures you can take to make the experience more relaxing.

If you can, fly or drive to the location the evening before. This is not always possible but try to do it if you can, even if you have to pay your own hotel expenses. You'll be more relaxed and ready for the event and will avoid the frustrations of traffic or flights that are delayed or cancelled. Go to the hotel and get a good night's sleep, or you can meet the interviewer for dinner and have a relaxing "getting-to-know-you" meal. It also gives you the chance to travel in casual clothes and change at the destination. This obviously keeps your clothes looking less wrinkled and unstained by the glass of tomato juice that could be spilled on you during a bumpy flight.

When you pack your bags, don't fold your clothes in a suit case if you can help it. If you must and they become wrinkled, hang them in the bathroom in your hotel room. Turn the hot water on and allow the steam to "iron" your clothes.

Always carry minimal luggage and carry it on the plane with you. It seems that the chances of an airline losing your luggage increase proportionately with the importance of the meeting, particularly if you're making a connecting flight or connecting with another airline. Carry your suit and dress shirt/blouse with you on hangers and pack your other items in a small carry-on bag.

If it's necessary to check your luggage, go directly to the airline counter rather than using the curb-side check-in. If you're running late for your flight, you can bring your luggage directly to the gate and still check it through to your destination.

If someone has arranged to pick you up, make sure you clearly know where you are to meet. To avoid miscommunications, always call to confirm the appointment time and location and to let the person know what color suit you will be wearing or offer some other way to recognize each other.

There are other means of identification. You could carry the company's literature with you or some other recognizable document. Perhaps the person meeting you could carry a sign with your name on it. You could also send your advance card ahead of you so the other party will more easily recognize you.

5) Interviews during a meal.

A more likely interview situation that you will be faced with is one held during a meal. It could be a relatively formal occasion where both you and your spouse are invited to meet with the company representatives, perhaps with their spouses. Or the meal could just be a logical extension of an interview that has gone over into the meal hour.

If your 10:30 am interview runs late and you and the interviewer are getting along well, she may ask you to join her for lunch. If so, you will probably be asked to name the kind of food you prefer. If you are short for time, you could say that a sandwich would be fine. If you know of a restaurant nearby that has a varied menu, use that as an indication of the type of restaurant you would enjoy. If you have any dietary restrictions, don't be embarrassed to say what they are.

When the time comes to order, let the interviewer order first and follow her lead. This doesn't mean you should order the identical item. It means to find out first if she orders an appetizer, salad, sandwich or something else that is quick to prepare. It could become embarrassing if the meal is significantly delayed because you ordered an appetizer, soup and salad and the interviewer didn't, or your well done steak took twenty minutes longer to prepare than her chef salad.

Since you'll be doing most of the talking, order a meal that is served cold so you can enjoy it at its proper temperature. Similarly, it's better to order something that can be cut into small pieces, rather than something that may require large bites, such as a club sandwich. Try to avoid spaghetti or other possibly messy items.

Other reasons to interview.

Most people have only one reason for interviewing, i.e., to get a job. But there are actually two other important reasons for interviewing. The first is to gain information, the second is to practice your skills.

1) The informational interview.

The informational interview is designed to help you gather information about career opportunities in different industries. You simply contact friends, industry leaders, alumni and colleagues and ask them to talk with you about careers in their field. The objective is not to get a job with them, but only to find out information that will help you make a decision about what career to enter and what types of jobs are available in it.

You are asking someone to serve as a temporary member of your Brain Trust. Make sure they know your intentions in advance and don't mislead them. Have a list of questions available that will elicit the information you need in the shortest amount of time.

2) The practice interview.

If you don't have experience interviewing, or have not done so in a few years, you should practice before you go on a critical interview. Simply respond to help-wanted ads as you normally would, but for positions in which you are not interested. Arrange interviews with prospective employers in which you can practice answering typical and atypical questions.

Prepare for each as you would for a "normal" interview. Dress appropriately and arrive on time. Practice answering questions, making your presentation and asking questions. Practice all the techniques for handling objections and asking and answering qustions that you'll learn in Chapters Nine and Ten. Make notes about areas in which you need more development, and then work to improve them later. Conduct the interview as if it was a "real" one, but don't mislead the prospective employer by feigning interest in the job. Cordially decline to come back for the second interview if asked to do so, and send the person a thank-you note as you normally would.

The interview life cycle.

Although your reasons for an interview will vary, you will find that each one goes through a pre-ordained series of stages. The length of each will vary, depending on where you are in the interviewing process for that specific job and your ability to participate in the discussion.

The interview process unfolds over a series of five separate stages. These are Preparation, Introduction, Presentation, Accumulation and Conclusion. There is no prescribed length of time that each of these will last. For example, on your first interview, you'll spend more time in the first three stages. As you move further along in the process with them, you'll spend more time in the latter stages.

STAGE ONE: PREPARATION.

The first stage occurs before you get in front of the interviewer. It is comprised of gathering all the information you need on your product and the company. It includes shining your shoes, ironing your blouse and practicing all the techniques that you will implement during the interview.

STAGE TWO: INTRODUCTION.

The second stage occurs when you first meet each other and engage in "small talk" to set each other at ease. Each party is "sizing up "the other, and the (generally) irrevocable first impressions are made. The length of this stage varies. On an interview with an experienced interviewer, the introduction will last long enough for him to make sure you are comfortable. With an inexperienced or nervous interviewer, this stage may be drawn out longer.

STAGE THREE: PRESENTATION.

This is the only stage in which you are "interviewed" according to the strict interpretation of the word. The interviewer is asking you questions and evaluating your responses to them. To communicate your benefits effectively, you must answer each question with a prepared presentation. Then you should probe to make sure the benefits were understood. If there is any misinterpretation or skepticism about your ability to provide these benefits, you must clear up that misunderstanding before you can proceed to another topic or stage.

STAGE FOUR: ACCUMULATION.

During this stage, the focus changes to the questions you have about the company. It is your chance to interview the interviewer. You have your criteria that a company should meet before you will accept the position, and you have a job description that will provide you with the greatest challenge and opportunity. Now you have to accumulate the information to find out how well this company and position match up against your ideal company and position.

STAGE FIVE: CONCLUSION.

Perhaps the most critical time in any interview occurs here. Too often, the interviewee allows the interview just to "end," instead of coming to a conclusion. You should have an objective before going on any interview. As the interview begins to wind down, you must ask for some commitment that will achieve your objective.

The sequence of interviews.

You will rarely be hired on the first interview. On the average, you'll go through three interviews before receiving an offer, each with its own "agenda" and each consisting of the five separate stages. However, the length of time spent in each stage will vary, as will the level of formality and apprehension.

You can view these changes as you would a continuum, moving from left to right. The first interview is more formal, structured and with greater emphasis on the early stages. As you move through the interviewing process, they will become less formal and structured. A graphic depiction would look like this:

First	**Second**	**Third**
Interview	**Interview**	**Interview**

Formal   Informal
Apprehensive   Relaxed
Structured   Unstructured
Emphasis on the   Emphasis on
  Early Stages   the Later Stages

1) The first interview.

<u>Your Objective</u>: Make a good impression and discern the extent to which the company and position meet your criteria. If that fit is good, you want to be invited back for another interview

<u>The Interviewer's Objective</u>: Uncover enough information to see if you have the necessary skills and personality, vis-a-vis the other candidates, to be invited back for a second interview.

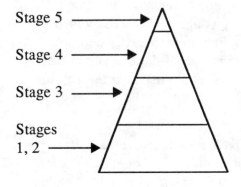

Stage 5

Stage 4

Stage 3

Stages 1, 2

The agenda for both parties in the first interview is to generate information upon which to base the decision on whether or not to proceed to the next step. The interviewer wants to eliminate those who looked good on paper but lack the "right stuff" to succeed in this particular position. The tone is more formal and it will tend to be more structured in nature. Your apprehension will be higher at this time than at any other time during the sequence, except for perhaps when it is getting time for the offer to come.

Stage One.

The emphasis rests on gathering information before you even attend the interview. You have to research the company and people as best you can to provide the basis for the questions you will ask in Stage Four.

Stage Two.

This will be the time at which your apprehension is at its peak, as you turn the corner into the interviewer's office. You both immediately size each other up and the initial impressions are made. This could be the most critical five minutes of the entire interview process, so it's important to practice all the elements of a successful approach.

Stage Three.

Perhaps the next 30 minutes or more will be spent in this stage. The interviewer will ask you questions, and you'll make your presentation to convince him that you have the skills to perform successfully on this job and offer more benefits than your competitors do.

Stage Four.

The length of time spent here will depend on the amount of information you gathered in Stage One and on your ability to ask questions. It will probably last at least the next twenty to twenty-five minutes.

Stage Five.

This will be relatively brief, since the level of commitment for inviting you back is not high on the part of either party.

2) The second interview.

Your Objective: Get answers to questions that came up since you had more time to "sift through" the information you obtained in the first interview, and if all conditions remain positive, make your first attempt at asking for the job.

The Interviewer's Objective: Introduce you to other people and determine the "chemistry fit" between the two of you and with the corporate philosophy.

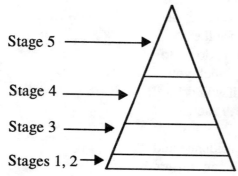

You will get the opportunity to meet with other people once you return. You must treat each one of those as your first interview. Before this occurs, you'll spend time with the initial interviewer, who will probably begin by asking you what questions have come up since you last met.

Stage One.

During the first interview you should have asked for more literature about the company to take with you and later read to get information about the company and its people and products. And from your notes about the first interview, you should have more ideas for potential questions to ask.

Stage Two.

This meeting will be more relaxed and you'll enter into small talk. Since you are now more familiar with the surroundings, you're probably more relaxed.

Stage Three.

Your presentation will be much more brief, both to your original interviewer and to any subsequent interviewers. You'll probably spend more time handling objections, since the other person has had time to think about what you said earlier and has had time to compare your benefits to those of your competitors.

Stage Four.

The transition into Stage Four will probably begin with the question "What questions have come up since we last talked?" and you'll spend the next half hour talking about your concerns. Or the interviewer may say, "Let me show you around." As you tour the office or production area, you'll be introduced to your potential co-workers. The questions will be less formal and directed more toward the specific department you are visiting at the moment.

Stage Five.

As your questions cease, or as you return to the interviewer's office, you'll have a fairly good "feel" for where you stand. You can tell by the more relaxed (hopefully) body language, and perhaps a request for your references. If you know that you want this job, you should say so. If you think it's appropriate to ask a committing question, do it now. Try to uncover any hidden objections that would prohibit you from coming back and get that commitment to return before you leave.

3) The third interview.

Your Objective: Get the job offer.

The Interviewer's Objective: Eliminate any areas in question and decide to whom the offer will be made.

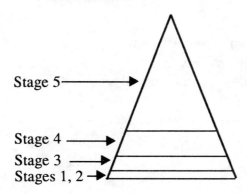

Your level of apprehension may rise a little at this time, because the list of contenders has come down to perhaps two or three, of which you are one. You know that if you do well you can get the job offer. Practice all your skills, and enter into this interview with all the confidence and positive feelings that you can muster.

Stage One.

Research any references the company gave you.

Stage Two.

More relaxed and informal greeting, perhaps over a cup of coffee in the cafeteria.

Stage Three.

If any questions came up while checking on your references, the interviewer will ask for clarification now. Also, any areas in which the interviewer feels uncomfortable will be addressed, and you'll have to handle them as objections unless they are simple misunderstandings.

Stage Four.

Ask any questions that linger to make sure you feel very comfortable accepting an offer if it is made.

Stage Five.

If the interviewer is vacillating because he is unsure about who should be given the offer, you'll spend more time in Stage Five asking direct and indirect committing questions. Don't leave without the offer if you really want it.

Your place in the sequence of interviewees.

When the interviewer calls you to arrange a time for the first interview, she will ask when it is convenient for you to come in. You have two options. You can arrange to be the first (or one of the first), to be interviewed, or you can ask to come in after the other candidates have been interviewed. As the Theory of Primacy and Recency states, you have a better chance of being remembered if you are first or last in a sequence of more than three.

If you decide to go in first, you can set the standard which future candidates must exceed in order to qualify. On the other hand, you won't have as much time to prepare yourself by gathering data on the prospective employer. You may also suffer from the "out of sight, out of mind" syndrome as the interviewing process goes on among the other candidates.

If you decide to go last, your benefits will have top-of-mind awareness among the interviewers. If it's been a long time since earlier contenders were interviewed, it's more likely that you could be the candidate of choice. You will also have more momentum going into the second round of interviews. It will probably be in your better interests to go in as late in the process as you can for your first interview, and as early as you can for the second interview. The second round will not take as long as did the first round, so you won't suffer from lack of recent exposure.

As you can see, many factors come to bear during each interview. The emphasis shifts, depending on the circumstances, but every stage is present during the entire process. The stages will now be discussed to give you a better feel for how you should handle yourself in each.

Stage One: Preparation

You will greatly enhance your chances for any job if you come across as having prepared for the interview. This includes practicing all the skills you will need. It also involves learning about the company before you arrive for the interview. You should be able to communicate the fact that you are applying to this particular company for a specific reason. You can't make it seem as if the interview is the result of haphazard circumstances. Similarly, there are many other areas in which you must prepare if you are going to score highly on your "test."

Gathering information on the company.

You should find out about the company before the first interview. Uncover what opportunities the company offers, it's recent growth, historical growth and any anecdotes which you can use in your approach. Look at their product line, industry trends, financial records (i.e., the annual report) and competitive position. If they have international holdings, what effect will the strength of the US dollar have on earnings and how safe are the foreign investments given the uncertain nature of world events?

Look for problems the company has, particularly in your sphere of influence. You can break these down into people problems (unions, management, personnel, etc.), growth problems (competition, sales, products, acquisitions, etc.) and functional problems (computer systems, procedures or production). Look for ways in which you can apply your talents to help the company solve these problems and bring these facts up in the interview. You may not want to offer a solution at this time but you do want to convince the interviewer that you have the skills to deal with the problems successfully.

There are several ways in which you can uncover this information. Have them send literature to you. Or if the company is nearby actually go there and ask the receptionist for product literature, company newsletters, annual reports and any other brochures that will provide you with background information. While you're there, ask for the proper spelling and pronunciation of the names of the people with whom you'll be interviewing.

If you need additional information, go to the library and look for the company's annual report. Check Dun and Bradstreet's listing for credit information. Then call friends in the business to determine the company's market presence and competitive position. Read the information in the directories that you initially reviewed during your prospecting efforts.

You should also re-read the classified ad that first attracted you to the position and bring it with you to the interview. Such ads generally contain a brief description of the company. When you are asked why you applied to their company, you can repeat the information given in the ad by saying you want to be employed by a "growing, dynamic industry leader" or however they described themselves in the ad.

Preparing your response to interview questions.

Properly answering questions is important to successful interviewing. If you show up unprepared, you'll find yourself waiting much longer than necessary to get the career position that is right for you. You have to prepare a response to typical questions that will be asked of you, and your presentation should demonstrate your benefits in that area.

You can use one of the following patterns to prepare your answers to questions. These are designed to provide you with a structure for your presentation, organizing it in a manner that is most persuasive, informative and conversational. Examples of these patterns are the following:

Chronological: This pattern involves a description of your education, experience or life style from the desired beginning point. Starting with the earliest relevant experience, you would describe each event before moving on to the next. Of course, the reverse-chronological presentation would begin with your most current activities and go backward in time.

Narrative: This format requires that you describe your skills and accomplishments in story format. You could, for example, tell how your semester at a college in Europe contributed to your education and overall maturity.

Enumerative: Make your response in the enumerative pattern when the interviewer gives you a list of performance criteria. You summarize the list and address each as a separate topic. For example, if the interviewer listed several character traits that he felt were critical to success, you would address each one and explain how you have demonstrated it in the past and how you would apply it in the future.

Geographical: When it is important to describe where something took place, you would use this pattern. If you have had experience both domestically and overseas, you could specify the advantages and disadvantages of each.

Prepare a response to the major questions listed in Exhibit 25 using these organizational patterns. Practice giving your response before you get into the interview situation, and you'll find yourself much more at ease answering the question when it comes up and presenting your benefits persuasively.

Final preparation.

The night before your interview, you should make sure you have everything you will need. Create a checklist to remind yourself to bring a pen, pad, your press kit, change for the parking meter, a copy of the letter you sent to the interviewer and extra copies of your resume. Don't assume that the interviewer will have the copy of the resume you originally sent him. You'll also find it helpful to have a resume with you when filling out the application. For the same reason, bring a list of your references, with their telephone numbers and addresses.

Always write down the phone number and address of the person you are going to see, and keep them handy. Searching for a telephone number or an address when you are running late or when you can't find a location can be frustrating.

You are what you wear.

There are many books on how to dress appropriately for an interview, written specifically for either men or women. You should read the appropriate one for more details. However, there are some basic requirements that you should understand.

First, be professional. Wear a conservatively colored suit or dress that has been freshly cleaned. The only exception to this would be on a second or third interview when the interviewer suggests you dress casually to meet for lunch on a Saturday or Sunday. If the interviewer does not suggest casual clothes, wear business attire. Check to make sure there are no buttons missing or tears in any seams.

Always take a shower before an interview, followed by an application of your favorite deodorant. Don't overdo make-up, perfume or after shave. It is better to have no scent than to have too much. Shine your shoes, coordinate the colors of your accessories, comb your hair and brush your teeth.

The Big Day!

The Big Moment has finally arrived, and it's time to leave for the interview. Always leave more than enough time to arrive early. Expect that there will be traffic or weather-related delays, or an accident that could hinder you. Don't drink coffee on the way to the interview; invariably you'll spill some on your clothes.

As you are driving to the interview, there is still more to be done. If it is an early morning interview, you should loosen up your voice by using an exercise from the Decker Communications program. According to their technique, say the vowels in order, each with a progressively deeper voice. Do this several times, then do it again placing an "M" before each vowel: "MA, ME, MI, MO, MU."

Relieving tension.

An important interview will always make you feel apprehensive, and you'll get the proverbial "butterflies in the stomach." As someone once said, it's normal to have butterflies, just make them fly in formation. A certain amount of nervousness actually sharpens your skills, as long as you keep it under control.

Dwelling on relieving nervous tension could increase your anxiety. Think instead about your strategy for the interview. Laughing at something will relax you. Make up your own personal morning credo and say it to yourself. Think back on all your successes and how good you felt as you experienced them. Convince yourself that you are well prepared and can handle anything that might come up.

Continue your exercises by doing "jaw stretches," i.e., alternately tightening and loosening your jaw muscles. You could also open your mouth as wide as you can, then relax it. Rotate your shoulders, and then relax them. Repeatedly tighten and loosen your fists.

Parking.

Once you arrive, try to find a parking place that is not in a tow zone or in the president's reserved parking space. You should devote your complete attention to the interview, not wonder whether your car will be towed. If you can, find an off-street place that's not in a metered zone. As you allocate time to get from your place to the interviewer's, allow a few extra minutes for finding a parking place.

Arriving at the office.

You should arrive in the reception area at least fifteen minutes before the time of the interview. If you expect to fill out an application form, you should provide even more time. If there is no traffic and you arrive earlier, use that time effectively. Wait out in your car and read material to brush up on the company's history or practice answers to the questions you expect to be asked. But in any event, don't ever be late for an interview.

If you tend to perspire more than most people, arriving late will only make it worse. You'll walk into the office dripping, due to both nervous tension and running to get there. Always arrive early enough for your body to adjust to the ambient room temperature before seeing the interviewer. Just in case, keep a clean handkerchief in each of your suits to wipe the perspiration from your face.

When you arrive, go directly to the lobby and announce your arrival to the receptionist in a confident way. If you have an outer coat and/or an umbrella, hang them up before you meet the person with whom you have the appointment. The receptionist will tell you where you can place them. It's always awkward to shake hands with a briefcase in one hand and a coat in the other. If you have time, go to the rest room and check everything out. Is your fly up? Any poppy seeds from that morning's bagel between your teeth? Hair combed? Tie straight? Slip showing? Get rid of your gum; then go back to the reception area and wait.

The application form.

While you are waiting to see your interviewer, you will probably be asked to fill out an application form. If you can, take it with you to complete it later, when you will be more likely to do so without making errors. Typing it makes it look more professional. If you must fill it out there, read through the application first, and then go back and complete it. Carefully print the information using a pen and keep it neat. If you perspire easily or are left handed, be sure you don't leave any fingerprints or smudge marks. Be accurate, honest, complete and as brief as possible. If you are in doubt about anything on the form, ask for an explanation. Have a copy of your resume and list of references (with addresses and telephone numbers) handy so that you can more quickly complete all the requested information. If asked to write a narrative about a topic, try to take it home so you can do it properly. Otherwise, make notes on your pad, then transcribe the information to the application.

Complete every blank space. If it doesn't apply to you (i.e., military service), indicate that in the space. Include your social security number, zip and area codes (even if your applying for a position in the same town). Regardless of where you complete the application, send or hand it unfolded and free of fingerprints to the person who originally gave it to you or to whomever you are directed to return it.

If you are applying for a secretarial position, you may be asked to take a typing test at this point. If other tests are to be used, they will most likely be given later in the selection process. These may be psychological or intelligence tests. Or they may be aptitude or dexterity tests, depending on the position.

If you are not given anything to do while waiting, do something to keep busy. Read the company's literature that is on the lobby table. If you can find the company's newsletter, read that right away. Find pictures of people and stories about the company's events that you can use later to help "break the ice." Don't put loose papers on your lap or they could fall off and create an awkward moment as you stand up and greet your host.

A secretary may lead you back to the interviewer's office. Make sure to greet her warmly and get her name. Ask questions about the interviewer, if you are unfamiliar with him. What are his hobbies? Does he have any children, and if so, what are their ages? Try to get the interviewer's business card, too. It will provide you with all the detailed information you need (title, spelling of the name, zip code, etc.) to send him a thank-you note later.

If offered coffee at this time, you should decline it. There's always the possibility of spilling it or placing the coffee cup down without a coaster on a desk. In any event, a coffee cup will just be one more unnecessary item in your hands to deal with when you greet your host.

Stage Two: Introduction.

As you arrive at the interviewer's office, thank the secretary warmly for taking you there. Use her name. Address every one as "Mr." or "Ms." until asked to do otherwise. Walk in confidently and look around for information with which to make your opening comments. Many people have an "ego wall" on which they hang all their plaques and awards. There may be a family portrait, a mounted animal on the wall or a special wall hanging. Is there a trophy the company soft-ball team won? Did one of their suppliers or customers recently give them some recognition? Maintain a constant awareness about the environment, and you will feel more comfortable in it.

Press the flesh but not too hard.

Shake hands with the interviewer, with a firm grip. If you tend to have sweaty hands, don't keep them in your pockets on the way to the interview. Keep a handkerchief with you to dry your hands just prior to the handshake.

Always shake hands with people upon first meeting them, whether male or female. Practice doing this at every opportunity. Learn to feel different grips and learn the appropriate grip for yourself. A firm handshake is much more desirable than a loose one, but a bone-crushing hand-shake is always undesirable. Stand a comfortable distance apart the first time you greet the person.

You should also learn how to receive a hand shake. Outgoing people will grasp your elbow or forearm with their left hand as they vigorously pump your right hand. If you relax your arm totally, you're in for a wild ride. After some people get to know you, they will put their left hand over yours to offer a warm, friendly greeting. They may even do this the first time they meet you to make you feel welcome and comfortable. Still others will offer their hand with the palm facing to the floor, which could cause awkwardness.

Wait to be shown to a seat, then take it gracefully. As you interview with people further up the organizational chart, you'll find that more and more offices are equipped with a sofa. While these appear more "homey" and less formal, it is difficult to maintain good posture while seated in a deep-cushioned couch.

Don't light up a cigarette. If the interviewer doesn't smoke, you take a great risk of alienat-ing him if you do. Even if the interviewer smokes, a variety of negative situations could occur. You could drop ashes on the carpet, the cigarette could roll out of the ash tray onto the desk, you could get smoke in your eyes, or you could drop the cigarette on your clothes. You can avoid any of these by refraining from smoking until you are back out in your car.

Body movement.

A visible factor that can indicate your confidence (or lack thereof) is your posture. Whether you are standing or sitting, your posture provides a good indication of how you feel about your-self. As you are interviewing, you can actually feel more confident by sitting up straight. Think to yourself, "How would I sit or stand right now if I knew I was on top of the world and nothing could get me down?" You will feel yourself straightening up, actually getting taller and conse-quently feeling more confident.

Don't slouch in the chair. If given the choice, choose a straight-back chair and keep your buttocks right in the 90 degree angle where the back and seat meet. But try to look (and feel) comfortable. A ramrod-straight back will make you appear stiff and unfriendly. Just find the posture in which you feel at ease and unbeatable and practice sitting and standing that way.

Posture is only one of the many features of body language that indicates feelings or moods.

Most of you are familiar with the more obvious ones, particularly folded arms, frowns, smiles and leaning back or forward. But their are other overt and less-overt moves of which you should be aware.

You don't have to be an expert in the science of body language but do maintain an awareness of the <u>changes</u> in body posture and facial expression in people. If you are unsure of the meaning behind a movement, ask the person. A comment such as "Did I say something to offend you?" will lessen the impact of the statement if you did.

People communicate more with their actions than with their words. Fidgeting or remaining unmovable will communicate nervousness even if you say you are calm. Change positions periodically so that you stay relaxed. Lean forward to emphasize a point, then lean back to listen. Look down and away periodically to reflect on a question before answering it. Then re-gain eye contact and lean forward to give your response.

I've found that jewelry salespeople use one very practical example of body language. When asked to show a pair of cuff links, for example, they will carefully take them out of the case and hand them to you as if they were worth a million dollars. You can use this same technique when handing a person your resume. Hold it at the top with one hand, then place your other hand underneath it to give it support. And hold it slightly higher than normal. Be careful not to drop it on the desk and push it over to the person. Make it look as if you are carefully handling a document that is important, because it is.

Eye communication.

There is one interviewing technique that you should adjust with different interviewers and it's the ability to control your eye contact with people. The word "control" is important because while some interviewers require heavy eye contact, others do not like it.

Some people are more visually oriented and will maintain eye contact longer than those who are not. You can tell who these people are right away. As you shake hands, they stare at you, almost testing to see if you maintain eye contact with them. They generally assume that if you don't maintain eye contact with them, you either have something to hide or you have an inferiority complex. But lack of eye contact is not necessarily an indication of either.

These same people also use phrases that suggest a visual orientation to life in general. Examples are "Get the picture," "From my perspective...," "Here's how I see it..." and "Show me what you mean." If you meet people who <u>speak</u> in visual terms, it's a good bet that you should maintain eye contact with them.

Other people do not feel comfortable with heavy eye contact, and you might do better avoiding it. When trying to make a point, look at the person with whom you are speaking, then look away for a moment to reflect on your next statement, thus giving the listener a mental break from the possibly intimidating feeling of eye "lock." If you use heavy eye contact with a person who feels uncomfortable with it, you will make the interviewer feel uneasy. He may terminate the interview to relieve the tension.

If you don't feel comfortable making eye contact at all, practice on yourself. Look into your own eyes in a mirror. Hold the contact for four or five seconds, then look away. Once you feel comfortable doing this, practice on young children. Then practice on your spouse, close friends and members of your Brain Trust.

Initiating the conversation.

    Your opening comments should seek to ease tension (especially yours), create a conversational tone and provide a smooth transition into Stage Three. At the same time, you want to gain the interviewer's attention and involvement. There are several techniques you can use to begin the interview. These include the following:

- **An interesting question**: "I read in this morning's paper that your company is opening a new plant. What impact will this have on this job?"

> Notice the reference to "this" job. You should make the transition from "this" job to "my" job midway through the first interview. Try to get the interviewer referring to the position this way, too.

- **A referral**: If you were referred to this position by a mutual contact, it is one of the strongest weapons in your career arsenal. The interviewer may not immediately recall that you are the one referred by his friend. Make sure the interviewer remembers that you are in fact this person. During your initial remarks, compliment your mutual friend and thank him, in his absence, for the referral (and always send a thank-you note to the referring person).

> There is a technique you can use to generate your own referrals. If you are turned down for the position, ask the interviewer if he knows of any other positions available that would meet your requirements. There may be another division in the company, or he may know of another company (a supplier, or customer) who needs someone with your talents. Always try to salvage some positive action from every interview.

- **An unexpected object**: You could hand the person a video tape and combine this with a question. For example, "Mr. Smith, do you have a VCR nearby? I would like to show you this video tape of the racing car that I designed."

- **A premium**: A premium is some small, attention-getting item. It could be a new product that you invented or some other relevant device. It could even be your personal career card with your resume printed on the back of it. As another example, you could show him the personal reply card he returned requesting that you call him. He would thus be reminded that you are the one who originally sent it.

- **An important piece of information**. "Mr. Smith, I did a great deal of research on your company's product line. I thought of a few ideas that might help you increase sales and at the same time cut costs. Would you like to hear about these ideas at this time?"

• **A compliment**: This must be sincerely presented, or it could come across as being phoney. If the person has on an attractive dress or nice tie, mention it to her or him. Try not to use this unless the situation warrants it. An opening comment should always be associated with the benefits you offer and help lead into your presentation.

Stages One and Two are very important to the overall success of your interview. These steps are generally overlooked because most job seekers want to get right into the "meat" of the interview and talk about their experience. They ignore the fact that some rapport must be established.

Take the time to find out about each opportunity, and let the interviewer know that this interview is important to you and is not like all the others. If he thinks that you are there simply because you are calling on companies alphabetically listed in the Yellow Pages, your chances of going further in the interviewing process are vastly reduced.

If you have adequately prepared yourself, the transition into Stage Three will go smoothly and positively. Just as your cover letter seeks to get the recipient to read your resume with positive anticipation, Stages One and Two do the same for Stage Three. And Stage Three does the same for Stage Four and Four for Five. Each builds upon the previous one and will be most effective if all the prior steps are successful.

The job search is not easy. You have to organize and prepare each one of the 100 things that can go right or wrong to make sure most of them go right. You have to practice perfectly in order to make your quest as short and productive as possible.

ASSIGNMENTS:

8.1   What are creative ways you can open the interview discussion? What items could you use as premiums to gain the interviewer's attention professionally?

8.2   What can you do to improve your eye communication, handshake and posture?

8.3   How can you create a response to typical interview questions using each of the presentation organization formats?

8.4   Who could you contact for an informational interview?

CHAPTER NINE

The Interview: Making Your Presentation

INTERVIEWING SKILLS

Handling Objections

Response Technique

List of Questions

STAGE THREE: PRESENTATION

After the initial warm-up period, Stage Three will begin. You'll feel the mood shift to "OK, now let's get down to business." The interviewer's tone of voice becomes more formal, and he will exhibit a shift in body movement, perhaps picking up your resume or application form. At this time (and depending on the type of interview), the interviewer will begin to ask you specific questions about your background, or ask you to describe your background to him.

This period is important because it's the interviewer's first time seeing you "in action." Once you begin, he will generally keep the interview going by asking a series of other questions to learn more about the "real you." These questions are intended to provide him with as much information as possible to make the right employment decision. The only data he has with which to make that decision is what you give him. Make sure that by the time you leave, you have provided everything he needs to know about you, in relation to his specific needs for an employee.

Too many candidates lose the job opportunity in Stage Three. Since they have come to the interview unprepared, they are expecting only to answer the questions presented to them. They sit back and wait for a question, briefly answer it, then wait for another question to be asked.

Take an active part in the interview.

You must actively participate in the interview: you cannot just answer questions. You should use your answers strategically to communicate your benefits in the most enticing way. You have to practice responding in a way that makes the interviewer realize that you have the best total benefit package of all the candidates. You must come across as an organized professional, who can communicate effectively.

Memorize a response technique, rather than a response.

There is a wide variety of questions you will be asked. Many can be anticipated, and your answers planned. But many unanticipated questions will be asked in response to your presentation vis-a-vis their specific needs. These are generally not the major questions for which you have prepared. Consequently, you will be more effective in answering questions if you can develop, practice and ingrain a <u>methodology</u> for responding and presenting that can be applied to a variety of questions. Here is such a sequence for you to follow:

EXHIBIT 24: TECHNIQUE FOR RESPONDING TO QUESTIONS

Step 1. Listen to the entire question without interrupting (especially if you "know" what he is going to say), and try to identify any hidden agenda behind it. Pause to organize your response.

Example: "Are you married?"

Step 2. If you are unsure of the intent or the substance of the question, ask for clarification:

"I'm not sure how that relates to my job performance. Could you explain what you mean?"

Step 3. Begin your response by rephrasing the question in a way that 1) demonstrates you understand the question, and 2) restates it in a way that is more conducive to your response:

"I see, Ms. Smith. So if I understand you correctly, you're concerned that my marriage may interfere with my ability to travel as much as will be required, is that correct?"

Step 4. Answer the question by making your presentation.

Making the presentation.

Once you have made a successful transition from the question, it's time to begin your presentation. You can use any of the presentation formats you developed during Stage One, depending on the direction you intend to take. Be careful not to make your answer too long, and always keep the interviewer involved in your response so it doesn't become a boring monologue. Remember to involve as many of the interviewer's senses (sight, sound, touch, taste and smell) as you can.

Refer back to the Seven Cs.

The seven communication guidelines apply to your verbal presentation as much as they do to your written correspondence. Speak in such a way that your answer is creative, credible, complete, current, convincing, concise and clear.

Looks can kill and so can your voice.

As you respond to the question, make sure to control your voice. By changing various aspects of your vocal presentation, you can express enthusiasm as well as substance in your response. There is an acronym you can use to remind yourself to control your voice properly. It is the word <u>SALARY</u>. Utilize the components of this acronym to create an attention-getting and captivating presentation.

<u>S</u>peed: Find the ideal rate of speech for yourself and begin each presentation with that rate. Change it as necessary to slow down when making a point and also to

improve your articulation. As a rule, try to match your rate of speech to that of the interviewer.

Accent: Emphasize particular words to give them more importance: "I <u>saved</u> my company <u>$5,000 a month</u> by designing a new computer system." Combine this with the appropriate body language to further accent your point.

Loudness: Adjust your volume to match that of the prospect. But if the interviewer becomes irate, don't antagonize him by raising your voice. Speak in a lower tone to help placate him.

Authority: Speak with authority and confidence. This will reinforce the impression that you are a professional and you know what you are talking about.

Rhythm: Adjust the cadence of your presentation, so you don't come across in a monotonous voice. Regularly adjust your volume, accent and rate of speech and try to match the needs of the situation at hand.

You: Speak in terms that are important to the interviewer. Refer to what is "of interest to you, Mr. Interviewer." Talk about the benefits you can bring to the interviewer's company.

Establish direction.

There are two techniques to help you lead smoothly into your presentation in response to the question. The first is a "Statement of Intentions," and the second is a "Funneling Statement." Both are designed to let the interviewer know that you are intent on answering the question to his satisfaction.

1) Begin with a Statement of Intentions.

A Statement of Intentions expresses exactly what you intend to accomplish with your answer. It's a good idea to begin the Statement of Intentions with a comment that helps position your response:

>*Ms. Smith, that's an excellent question. In fact, there are several reasons why my being married is particularly well suited to meeting the travel requirements you described. Let me begin by explaining what I mean.*

2) Or use a Funneling Statement.

You can also use the Funneling Technique to relate the conversation immediately to a point the interviewer previously made. It starts out with a broad statement of something important to the interviewer, then makes the transition into the specific part of your background that relates to the interviewer's need. For example:

>*Mr. Jones, as you stated earlier, a major trait contributing to successful sales-manship is persistence. As this letter demonstrates* (hand it to him), *my customer feels that I have professionally exhibited tenacity and determination in a variety of situations. Let me begin by telling you how this letter came about.*

Use all the tools at your disposal.

Use audio and visual aids if appropriate. And use your press kit to help you methodically move through the presentation. If you have prepared it in the proper order, it will unfold as a logical, comprehensive portrayal of your skills and benefits. If you are showing a portfolio of your creative accomplishments, you don't have to review every piece with the interviewer. Just show representative samples of your performance and the results that were achieved. Make sure you emphasize the <u>strategy</u> that was behind the implementation, not just the end result.

If there is a blackboard or flip chart in the room, stand up and write on it. If nothing else, it will serve as a reminder of your presentation after you leave. Show photographs, reference letters, testimonials or perhaps even a sample of a product you developed. Use your presentation to keep the interviewer focused on the benefits you can bring to the company.

Always support the interviewer's positive remarks.

Address each question as it comes up. And before going on to the next question or topic, get the interviewer's commitment that he agrees your specific accomplishments would be very beneficial to the company.

> *And so, Mr. Jones, these letters testifying to my presentation abilities, and the*
> *video tape of my most recent group presentation demonstrate my platform skills.*
> *Do you agree that these skills will be of great benefit to me as your Director of*
> *Human Resources?*

If he says "Yes," agree with and support his reply, reinforcing in the interviewer's mind the value you can bring to this position. Simply follow his statement with a phrase that augments it, such as "You're absolutely right" or "Exactly." Then go on to the next criterion.

> *I agree, Mr. Jones. Now, as I recall, you said the second major qualification for*
> *this position is _____, right? Let me show you how I ...*

Handling skepticism.

On the other hand, if he appears skeptical and doesn't readily agree with your statement, it's important to bring that out into the open and address it now. You will not get an offer as long as any lingering doubt remains in the back of his mind.

As you address a negative response to your question, use this sequence:

1) Find out where he thinks you are lacking in the ability to meet this requirement. Ask "Oh? Why?" or "Why not?"

2) Then show that you recognize his concern, but not that you agree with him ("I <u>understand</u> what you are saying, Mr. Jones, but...").

3) Offer some additional proof about your ability to meet his needs ("If you look at it this way...").

4) Then draw a conclusion and ask for his commitment that he now agrees you actually do meet his criterion for that qualification ("So this demonstrates that I can perform that function. Don't you agree?").

Handling objections.

The interviewer may be more than just skeptical about your statements. He may more strongly object to something that you said, because of either misunderstanding or disbelief. When this occurs, there are additional methods to use that will address this stronger feeling of objection.

These techniques will be more effective if you first distinguish between an objection and a question. If an interviewer says, "Do you have a graduate degree," he is asking a question, and you should just answer it. If you don't have a graduate degree, ask if that is a critical condition for the position. If he responds by saying "We only hire MBAs," that is an objection.

When to handle objections.

There are two times when it is best to handle such a situation. First, you should address the concern before it comes up, and secondly, when it comes up during the interview.

A) Anticipate objections.

The best time to handle an objection is before it comes up. By anticipating a possible objection to your employment, you can prepare a presentation that will make the perceived negative sound like a positive. Don't automatically bring up reasons for the interviewer to reject you, but if you are regularly stymied because you feel you are too old, too young, too inexperienced or too anything, you have to deal with such objections in the interview:

> *Mr. Jones, I don't have a great deal of on-the-job experience. However, I do have twenty two years of experience being an honest and trustworthy person. I've also had sixteen years of experience with formal education, demonstrating my leadership skills through participation in extra-curricular activities. During this time, I had four years of experience at college balancing a budget, while meeting my financial obligations as I had promised to do when the lenders trusted me with their money.*

> *Through four years of college, I demonstrated an inquisitive nature that will help me continue my education with a fervor that people who have been on the job for many years cannot recapture. And I have experience approaching new opportunities with an open mind, willing to apply creative techniques for solving problems others thought were insurmountable.*

> *Mr. Jones, isn't that the kind of experience that would make me successful with this company?*

OR (if you don't have a college degree),

> *Mr. Jones, I'm one of the many people who has demonstrated success even though they don't have a college degree. And I look at success under these circumstances as a benefit. Many college students graduate with the feeling that the answer to any problem can be found in a textbook. If there is no logical answer for it there, they may think it can't be done.*

> *I always approach a tough situation by viewing it as a challenge which I know I can overcome. I assume there is an answer for every problem, and I just have to*

find it. Thus I approach every challenge with determination and optimism. Isn't that what you're really looking for in a salesperson Mr. Jones?

If you regularly feel you are being rejected because you are too old, think of ways to present "maturity" as a welcome asset. You "know the ropes," you've had twenty years of successful experience, and you can save the company a lot of money that it would otherwise have to spend training younger people. You could also relate that you are "politically savvy," which is something your younger competitors cannot say.

As a caveat here, don't assume you are "too anything." You'll get yourself into trouble if you presuppose you don't have a particular qualification. It might even become a self-fulfilling prophecy. In your self-evaluation, determine the areas which you need to strengthen. Then as you are working on them, anticipate in your presentation possible objections that might come up about them. If you address your "perceived" weakness in a positive way, you can usually find a benefit that will overcompensate for it.

For example, handling objections based on price.

If you know you are asking for more money than the position offers, you should have several responses prepared to combat this objection. You could try the following:

- Demonstrate the difference between "price" and "cost." To them, the salary level is the "price." The "cost" of hiring you will be much less if you can immediately be productive. Prove you can help them lower their overall costs in an amount greater than your income. And demonstrate that the benefits you offer will more than compensate for the money you require.

- Discuss only the <u>incremental</u> cost. If they offer an annual salary of $30,000 and you require $35,000, talk about the difference. Don't try to justify the larger amount, i.e., $35,000. Discuss only the $5,000 difference and prove that your skills and subsequent benefits to the company are worth much more than that amount.

- Break the difference down to its smallest incremental amount. If you are trying to get $5,000 more per year, that is only $96 per week and only $2.40 per hour. When you present your benefits in terms of $2.40 per hour, they seem more reasonable.

B) Handle objections as they come up.

Of course, there will be unexpected objections that surface during the interview. These must be handled at that time, or the interviewer may think you are trying to avoid answering them. You can more effectively handle these if you again have a "method" for handling objections in general. The following techniques will provide you with this methodology.

Get <u>READY</u> to handle objections.

A formula which you can use to handle these objections is called the **READY** formula. It was developed by Joel Weldon on his cassette program called "The Million Dollar Attitude" (Nightingale-Conant Corporation, 3730 West Devon Avenue, Chicago, IL 60659). **READY** is an acronym that provides a framework for thinking on your feet and handling objections for which you have no prepared response:

Reverse it: Try to catch the interviewer off guard by making her objection the reason for hiring you. "That's right, Ms. Smith, I do request $5,000 more than you offered, and that's exactly the reason you should hire me." Then go on to explain how the $2.40 per hour difference is a bargain for the Phi Beta Kappa product you are selling.

Explain it: "The reason I didn't go to college immediately after high school is that I couldn't afford it since I needed additional income to support my family. But let me show you what I have done to continue my education while I earned the money to return to night school...."

Admit it: "That's correct, Ms. Smith, I don't have any work experience. But I do have an open mind and a sincere desire to learn your company's ways of doing things. My lack of experience will actually be beneficial because I don't have any pre-conceived notions about how things should be done. Isn't that important, Ms. Smith?"

Deny it: "Actually Ms. Smith, that's not correct. I wasn't fired from that job. In fact, here is a reference letter written by the president of that company." You have to be delicate handling an objection this way, because you don't want to create an atmosphere of confrontation or the feeling you are out to prove the interviewer wrong. If you can, take the blame for not describing that situation more clearly. Diffuse the situation without accusing the other person of any guilt. Look at it as just a misunderstanding that must be clarified.

Yes, and...: Agree with the statement and use that as the reason for hiring you. "Yes Ms. Smith, I have more than twenty years of experience in this industry. And that's exactly why you should hire me. Here, let me show you what I have done to...."

The Home-Buyer's Technique.

Another system for handling objections is called the "Home-Buyer's" technique. As you would expect from its name, it's analogous to the process of buying a house. People spend many days and weeks looking for the "perfect" home, thinking it is out there somewhere. In the process, they may pass up many fine homes that don't have everything that they want but that meet many of their other criteria. Later they realize that there is no such thing as a "perfect" house and that they'll have to make trade-offs.

In your job search, this technique recognizes there is no perfect employee (or employer), and even allows an objection to remain if it is impossible to surmount. You grant that it exists but present benefits that over-compensate for the perceived deficiency. It is difficult to change someone's mind when he is wrong, and wrongful to try and change his mind when he is right.

For example, an interviewer may want to hire someone who is over six feet tall, for whatever reason. If you are not six feet tall, there is nothing that you can do to change this situation. You have to allow for that fact while introducing benefits that will make you more valuable to the company than the taller candidate. Don't try to minimize or eliminate the criterion. Allow it to exist, but show that you have something more important to offer that the taller person may not have.

A tried and true technique.

One alternate way to handle an objection is to use the Feel/Felt/Found method. You begin by stating that you understand how the interviewer <u>feels</u>, thereby trying to reduce any conflict (understanding how he feels doesn't mean you agree with him). Then you let him know others have <u>felt</u> that way, so he knows that you have come up against this before. Then once you have created this atmosphere of openness, you tell him how others have <u>found</u> the opposite to be true and why. Close the topic by asking a question that gets him to agree with you.

As an example, suppose the interviewer just told you he wanted to delay filling the open position for two months, until the new budget period begins. You obviously would prefer to start now. You could respond with something similar to the following:

> *I understand how you <u>feel</u>, Mr. Jones. Other companies have <u>felt</u> the same way. But what they <u>found</u> was that if a person was hired just prior to the end of a budget period, he could complete his plans during this relatively slow holiday period. That way he could begin the new year with a head start. This translated into earlier success and results, making a traditionally slow first quarter the best ever. Doesn't that sound like the results you would like to see happen for this company?*

Lower the commitment level.

This last technique for handling objections is to lower the commitment level expected by the interviewer. It should be used when you are deficient in a certain area and your other attempts at convincing the interviewer to the contrary haven't worked. The drawback to this method is that it requires you to lower your objective at the same time. You have to look at it as a short-term investment, with your eye still on your long-term mission statement.

If you implement this technique, you have to take a cut in pay or reduce some other factor in order to make yourself more competitive for the position. If you are in great need of a job or really want to work for this specific company, then this technique could be beneficial to you. For example:

> *Mr. Jones, I feel strongly that I could make an excellent contribution to your revenue as your Vice President of Sales. But I don't have the line-management experience that you require. However, I do recognize the long-term opportunity this company offers, and I would be willing to start out as your Regional Manager in order to gain the experience you require. Which of your regions needs the most help now?*

Always get commitment.

After each attempt at handling an objection, you should ask a question to get agreement with what you said. If the interviewer doesn't agree, you must find out why not, and then handle that as another objection. You have to clear up any misunderstanding or you won't get the offer. If the interviewer agrees with your handling of the objection, offer a support statement and go on to the next topic or question.

Exhibit 25 lists questions that you could be asked by an interviewer. You have to anticipate a response to these questions in such a way as to best present your accomplishments. Other questions may well be asked of you, but if you have practiced the technique for properly answering questions, you'll be better prepared to handle them and the possible objections that your answers could create.

EXHIBIT 25: QUESTIONS INTERVIEWERS WILL ASK YOU

Who (other than your parents) has influenced your life the most? How?

Why shouldn't we hire you?

What is your description of unethical conduct?

What are two challenges that you have successfully met? How?

Why should I pay you more than what I've just offered?

What are your long- and short-term objectives?

How do you spend your spare time? What are your hobbies?

In what types of positions are you most interested?

Describe your perfect job.

Why do you think you would like to work for our company?

How did you happen to apply to this company?

What do you know about this company?

What jobs have you held? How were they obtained?

Why did you leave each of your previous jobs?

What did you learn most from each previous job?

What did you like/dislike most about each of the jobs you have had?

Why did you choose this particular field of work?

What do you think determines a person's progress in a company? How do you meet these criteria?

What personal characteristics are necessary for success in your chosen field? How do you rate yourself against each?

Do you prefer working by yourself or with others?

What kind of supervisor do you prefer?

How was your attendance at school/on the job? Why were you absent?

What makes you feel successful? Define success.

How do you take instruction/criticism?

How do you want to be remembered (The "Tombstone Test," i.e., what inscription do you want on your tombstone)?

How have you continued your education since leaving school? (Or how do you plan to continue your education after leaving school?)

Who is your favorite fiction author?

What were your favorite subjects in school? In what subjects did you do best? Worst?

How did you choose your major? College?

How would your best friend (or spouse) describe you?

Can you get recommendations from your previous employers? How would they describe you?

What interests you about our product or service?

What do you know about opportunities in the field for which you are trained?

How do you feel about overtime? Travel?

What are your strong points? Weak points?

Do you need or desire close supervision?

How do you approach solving a problem?

What makes you think you can succeed in this position? Company?

Tell me about yourself.

Do you consider yourself to be creative?

How long do you plan to stay with this company?

What do you have to offer this company?

What part of the newspaper do you read regularly?

How is your health? Any disabilities that would prohibit you from successfully performing in this position?

What is your most important personality trait?

What is your weakest personality trait? What have you done to strengthen it?

What are you doing to try to find a job?

How did you choose your last (present) employer? What went wrong (i.e. why do/did you want to leave)?

What jobs did you have while going to school?

How much of your college expenses did you pay?

What is your most significant accomplishment? Why?

What are/were your parent's occupations?

What do you want to be doing in ten years? Twenty years?

What makes you feel happy? Angry?

In what extra-curricular events did you participate in school? Any special honors?

What motivates you? What doesn't motivate you?

What kind of car do you drive?

What did you like/dislike about your previous supervisors/teachers?

Did you write your resume or did someone do it for you?

How would your worst enemy describe you?

How do you organize your time?

Do you speak any foreign languages fluently?

What career-related books have you read recently?

Define cooperation. Teamwork. Office politics. Loyalty. Etc.

Is there anything else you want to tell me?

Honesty.

As the interviewer asks you questions, you may be tempted to answer with what you think he wants to hear. Don't do it. You must answer every question honestly. You have to answer with what _you_ feel, because once you get the job and perform it in your own way, the fact that you were misleading will become obvious.

Working with a company is much like getting married. You can enter into the relationship thinking you can change the other party or that you can change to meet the other's expectations. Neither case will work out in the long run. After an initial "honeymoon" period when both sides are trying to make it work, the _real_ personalities of both sides will emerge.

Discriminatory questions.

There is one area that could cause problems on an interview and that is discriminatory, illegal or problematic questions. Under federal law, an interviewer can ask you any question, as long as it is asked of <u>all</u> interviewees (both male and female), <u>and</u> it is related to a documented qualification for the job. It would be legitimate for an interviewer to ask about your marital status if he was concerned about your freedom to travel or relocate. It would not be legitimate to ask the same question if there was an ulterior motive. It is the implication or intent of the question that would make it illegal or not and whether it was asked of both men and women.

You should anticipate how you would handle questions such as "Do you want more children?" or "What type of child-care will you use?" or "What would your husband say if you were transferred?" If you are asked a question that you think is discriminatory or illegal, try to determine its intent from the way it was asked. Don't immediately take a defensive stance, for the question may be a legitimate concern related to the proper performance of the job. A question like "Oh, you have a daughter? How old is she?" may just be a way to build rapport if the interviewer has a daughter of perhaps the same age. Or, depending on the intent, it could be an inquiry into how frequently you'll be off the job taking care of a sick child. If you're unsure of a question's intent, simply respond with, "I'm not sure how that relates to my job performance. Could you explain what you mean?"

If you use the techniques demonstrated here, the hour or so that you spend together will be mutually informative. The interviewer will understand more about you and the unique benefits you can bring to his company. At some point in the conversation, he will cease to ask anymore questions and begin the transition to Stage Four. Then it is your turn to find out more about the company and the specific opportunity.

ASSIGNMENTS:

9.1 Review the list of questions in Exhibit 25 and prepare possible responses to each. What other questions might be asked of you based on your specific field of interest?

9.2 What objections do you regularly hear regarding your education or experience (or lack thereof)? How can you anticipate these and turn them into reasons for hiring you?

CHAPTER TEN

Interview The Interviewer

When the interviewer has exhausted his list of questions, he'll move into Stage Four by beginning to describe the company in general and the position itself in more detail. At this point, the burden of asking question shifts to you. Too many interviewees lose a tremendous opportunity here as they just sit back and listen to the descriptions. Many times they are not listening but just <u>hearing</u> the words, glad that their participation in the interview is over.

Have the interviewer fill out an application.

You must remember that the interview is not just a time for the prospective employer to learn about you. It is also your chance to find out if the company and the opportunity at hand are the best ones for you, given your specific objectives. You are betting your career on the job, so you must make sure you have sufficient information with which to make the right decision. In effect, you should ask to see the resume of your manager-to-be and also that of the company. Have your own "application form" in mind and have the prospective employer complete it by answering your questions.

Ask for the company's references.

If you aren't sure about something, ask. If you want to find out more about something, ask. Find out what references the company has and later contact them. Ask for a list of customers, current employees and even past employees who you could contact. The company will probably ask for and check your references and they should expect that you will do the same.

A long-lasting career must begin with a win/win situation. Unless you and your employer are satisfied that this is the right opportunity for both parties, doubts will linger. You must ask questions that get the interviewer to expose any hesitation, so you can eliminate it before you leave. If any uncertainty remains after your departure, your chances of being asked to return are reduced.

You need to make sure your manager-to-be is wholeheartedly behind your candidacy. <u>You</u> must make sure the interview is a <u>mutually</u> satisfying event. A monologue by either party will not accomplish that. You must take the initiative to become involved and remain involved in the discussion. As the interviewer gains more information about and confidence in you, he is more likely to be convinced that you are the best person for the job.

The following quotation addresses the importance of getting the other party involved and getting him to sell himself on you. It re-affirms the need to make the decision a win/win situation through mutual involvement:

> **One convinced against his will,**
> **is of the same opinion still.**

This quotation doesn't mean that a prospective employer will hire you even though he doesn't want to. It suggests that some people will make a decision "against their better judgement" because they can't place a finger on the area in doubt. As you learn to ask committing questions, you'll be better able to uncover any points that are in question and deal with them so the interviewer is satisfied that you will do the best job.

Your objective for the interview should be to get the decision maker to <u>sell himself</u> on you as the best candidate. You can do this through the use of effective questions that are strategically phrased. Then as the interviewer answers them, he will in effect convince himself of your ability to perform better on the job than can your competition. Therefore, the above quotation can be amended with the "Jud Corollary" to make it read:

> **One convinced against his will,**
> **is of the same opinion still.**
>
> **But those convinced by what they say,**
> **will sell themselves and stay that way.**

STAGE FOUR: ACCUMULATION

This stage of the interview process pertains to a discussion of the company (its history, size, organization, philosophy) and the details of the job for which you are applying. It's now your turn to ask the questions and have the interviewer present his case to you. He in effect has to sell you on the benefits of the company and how they can meet your long-term needs.

The questions you ask at this point are very important. They offer insight into your needs, since you will obviously ask about areas that are of interest to you. In turn, the interviewer will explain how the company can meet your needs in that area. If you ask questions about the benefits the company offers, the interviewer will stress the company's insurance and pension plans. He'll recognize the company's primary and secondary benefits vis-a-vis your specific criteria. And if he really wants you, he may even offer a "grabber" to give you an incentive to accept. His "grabber" might be a three-week vacation after five years of employment.

It should be obvious to you now that your involvement in Stage Four is important to fulfilling your job-related needs. The questions you ask will direct the interviewer's presentation, just as his did your presentation. This will impact both the quality and quantity of information you will have upon which to base your decision.

How to ask questions.

There are other ways in which you can strategically use questions to your advantage in an interview. You can use them to get the interviewer to reveal needs, hidden objections and even additional opportunities. You can use them to give yourself time to think, check on your understanding of a situation or demonstrate your knowledge of a situation. And you can utilize them to keep both parties involved in the discussion.

Two major categories of questions are "Focusing" questions and "Expansion" questions.

The first type is designed to direct the topic of conversation or briefly check your understanding of a comment. They elicit a relatively quick answer. It may be a "yes" or "no," or it could be a choice between two alternatives that you supply.

The second type is designed to get the interviewer to expand on a topic so you can learn more about it. And the more the other person talks, the more likely it is that he or she will reveal hidden objections, needs and opportunities, in addition to satisfying your needs for information.

1) Focusing questions.

These questions are designed to direct the conversation to an area of importance to you. For example, from your research into the company before the interview, you should have determined topics in which you had questions. If the conversation begins to lead away from these issues, you must re-direct the flow back to your area of interest.

There are different types of questions that can help you focus:

Dichotomous questions. These ask for a simple "yes/no" answer. They provide a good lead-in to more detailed questions, as well as specific answers. Generally nothing is lost in the translation of the answer, but dichotomous questions can enable the interviewer to make a choice between two alternatives or to accept your inquiry on a specific topic.

For example, you could say "Does the company have a 401K program?" The answer would be "Yes" or "No." It also opens the door to further questions in the area of benefits. Once your information needs are satisfied on that topic, you could ask, "Will I be required to travel on this job?" Your follow-up question could then open the discussion to the extent of time you'll be expected to spend "on the road" or the company's expense policy.

Closed-response questions. These seek a specific answer that cannot be a "yes" or "no." It should be used to direct the topic of conversation and followed by a question to get the interviewer to explain his answer.

For example, if you asked, "What is the single most important trait that would lead to my success on this job?" You would then follow the answer with "Why is that?"

Multiple-choice questions. A question that offers a list from which the interviewer may choose an answer is useful but dangerous. You shouldn't presuppose that the interviewer doesn't have other possible alternatives. Always qualify your list and ask the interviewer if he has others to add.

For example, you could ask, "Your ad said you are looking for a person with analytical, financial and communication skills. Which of these do you feel is the most important?" (Wait for the answer.) "Why?" (Wait for the answer.) "What other criteria would you add to the list?"

2) Expansion questions.

Once you direct the discussion to a specific topic, you should get the interviewer to expand on his initial answer. Expansion questions are designed to keep the interviewer talking and providing additional information. They generally begin with words or phrases such as "Who, What, Where, When, Why, How, Tell me more about ..., In how many more ways can ..., etc."

Most of the questions in Exhibits 25 and 26 are expansion questions. They allow for both direction and magnitude of interest and provide the opportunity for the respondent to open up and express more of the reasoning behind his answer.

Strategically, you should follow the answer to a focusing question with an *expansion* question. Here are a few examples of using this questioning technique:

Is there a high turnover rate among your employees? Why?

Do you promote from within? Why not?

Does success in this position require a college degree? Why do you feel that way?

Does the company support continuing education for its employees? What do you do to encourage this?

Exhibit 26 offers a list of questions you can use as a starting point for your inquiries. Create your own list of questions that will elicit the information you need in order to make an informed decision for your particular situation and goals. Add questions that will uncover details about your specific job responsibilities. Use the job description you created earlier to stimulate your thoughts. You should also review your checklist of employer criteria to create questions that will help you determine the company's ability to meet your "demands."

EXHIBIT 26: QUESTIONS YOU CAN ASK AN INTERVIEWER

What are the most important responsibilities of the position?
How will my success be measured against these responsibilities?
What is an example of a typical career path, beginning with this position?
What type of person succeeds in this position? Company?
What is your management style (if talking with your manager-to-be)?
What are the company's strengths? Weaknesses?
How are raises determined (Consumer Price Index? Longevity? Performance?)
What are the company's long-term growth plans? Internal growth or through acquisitions?
What type of feedback (reviews) can I expect? Frequency?
What kind of training can I expect? When?
How does the company feel about paying for ongoing education?
What is the company's image among its customers? Competitors? Suppliers?
What is the turnover rate among company personnel? Why?
Why is this position open? What happened to the previous incumbent?
What exactly will I be expected to accomplish in the next year? Two years? What will be the reward if I exceed these goals?
What new products were introduced in the past two years? What about next year?
What other divisions/subsidiaries are there in the company? Are there opportunities for my future growth in these?
What income could be expected two years from now? Five years?
What are the opportunities for an equity position in the future?

How are budgets determined? Monitored?

What is the historical compound asset/equity growth? Historical growth in ROI (Return On Investment)? Average return on equity? Average return on sales?

What other markets are available for growth in which the company is not presently participating?

What portion of the total sales are derived from international operations? Are there opportunities for my future growth internationally?

How much autonomy will I have?

What is the company's current market share? Expected share?

What does the company do that is different and better than what competitors are doing? What could we be doing?

What are the industry trends for the markets in which the company participates?

What does the company do to communicate to the market (advertising)?

What kinds of computer reports are available for tracking results?

(For a sales position) What are the territory boundaries for which I will be responsible? What is the history of the territory? What is the future of the territory? How is my quota determined? What percent travel is required to achieve superior performance? How are expenses handled? Travel budgets? Car allowance? Competitive activity in the territory? Price cutting? Performance measurements? Customer service? Field support? What literature is currently available? (Ask to take samples of literature with you.)

Tell me about upper management, i.e., growth philosophy (from internal products or acquired), attitude toward employees, downward communication, delegation and promotion from within?

What is the attitude of the production people regarding quality? How is this measured?

How are new ideas sought? Acted upon? Rewarded?

What is the background of the upper managers?

Oh? Why do you say that? (In response to a statement by the interviewer about which you would like more information.)

How do you motivate people?

What does this company do to encourage attitudes of independence and self-reliance among its employees?⁻

How would you define the company's personality (Entrepreneurial? Stable?)

What incentives are provided to reward superior achievement?

With whom may I speak for more information about you? The company?

Ask questions that will uncover the company's ability to provide the benefits and other criteria that you have determined.

Ask questions to find out how the job description for the position matches the "perfect" job description you wrote.

Should I start next Monday, or should I wait until the fifteenth?

Ask questions strategically.

There is an art to asking questions properly. You can't appear to be "challenging" the person when you ask a question. When you follow with "Why?" to the respondent's answer, you must couch it with proper body language so it doesn't come across in a defiant or demanding way. Instead of a direct "Why?" you might say "Oh, why do you say that?" or something similar.

You don't want the interview to appear as an interrogation. Ask one question at a time and listen to the answer. As you can see, strategy is critical to your success in using questions to participate in the interview and making sure you find out everything you need to know to make an informed decision. Ask each question as if it is the only one you intend to ask. Then listen to the answer.

An alternative to working from a list of questions enables you to glance down at your pad and be reminded of questions without having to stop to read from a long list. Simply write down the general areas in which you want information; then use subheadings to remind yourself of specific topics about which to inquire. Then as you ask each, cross it off. Your notes could look like the following:

JOB CONTENT	COMPANY	OPPORTUNITY	MANAGER-TO-BE
Responsibilities	Strengths	International	Turnover rate
Measurement	Weaknesses	Other divisions	Management style
Future	Benefits	Other departments	
Feedback	Growth trends	Career paths	
Budgets	New products	Incentives	
Travel	ROI		

Remember these hints when you're asking questions.

Whether you're using focusing or expansion questions, there are important points to keep in mind:

- Use leading questions to get the interviewer to reveal her needs. Then lead the discussion so that you can satisfy these needs with the benefits you have to offer. If you speak fluent French, you could ask:

  > *Do you think it would be important for your inter-national operations manager to speak French fluently?*

- Leading questions are also effective when you are at the point where you want to ask for the job. You would follow a positive response with a support statement and a request to begin working. A negative response would be handled as an objection.

  > *Don't you agree that my background exactly matches the qualifications you were seeking in the ad?*

- Use expansion questions to find out exactly what attributes the interviewer is looking for:

  Interviewer:

  > *I'd like to get a person with (whatever) experience but I guess that person just doesn't exist.*

You:

> *Oh? Why do you say that?*

• The interviewer may not tell you the areas in which she thinks you are deficient. You must ask questions to get her to reveal hidden objections or possibly negative attitudes toward your candidacy. You would then respond by handling them as objections. For example, if you did not attend graduate school, you might probe into her feelings about that fact:

> *What level of formal education do you think is required for success in this position?*

• Don't ask more than one question at a time or the interview will sound like an interrogation and reduce rapport. Here is an example of what not to say:

> *What are the strengths and weaknesses of the company, and what is the company doing to improve its market position?*

• Use expansion probes to give yourself time to think of an answer or to help you determine what the interviewer is really getting at:

> *Why do you ask that?* or *Why is that much experience absolutely necessary for success in this position?*

• Use focusing questions to check your understanding of a situation:

> *If I understand you correctly, all future raises are based upon the Consumer Price Index rather than individual performance. Is that what you're saying?*

• Posing a hypothetical question is useful to demonstrate your understanding of the situation, and at the same time it shows that you are using your creativity:

> *Just suppose (describe your idea). What would that do to the company's sales volume?*

> *What if (offer some alternative course of action)?*

• Use questions to keep the flow of information going:

1) Give a brief assertion of interest or a sign that you are interested in what the interviewer is saying and you want to hear more about it:

> Oh, really?

> *That's very interesting. Could you please expand on that point?*

2) Provide a reflective response, one in which you mirror your understanding of the interviewer's feelings without implying that you necessarily agree:

I can understand why you feel a graduate degree
would be important in this position, but have you
looked at it from the perspective of...?

3) Many people feel uncomfortable with silence, and they tend to fill in silent space with additional comments. Therefore silence can actually be useful in lieu of a question to keep the conversation going. This technique will be more effective if you use body language to reinforce your pause. You could tilt your head, raise your eye brows, and give an understanding nod to show that you want her to keep talking.

• <u>Neutral questions</u> can help you learn about the interviewer's particular application without admitting you know nothing about it:

How does that new accounting technique differ
from what you were using before?

• Use <u>focusing questions</u> to get agreement with your point of view without proving the interviewer wrong. If you do the latter, you could win the argument and lose the job offer.

Try to provide additional salient information that will help demonstrate your point. Giving him a rational reason to change his mind will allow him to do so without losing "face." After you've given him more details, ask a committing question that is posed in an un-challenging manner:

If you look at it from that perspective, my experi-
ence in the market could be more important to the
company than an inexperienced person with an
MBA, couldn't it?

STAGE FIVE: CONCLUSION

Once you have exhausted all your questions, the interview will begin to enter Stage Five. The interviewer will usually summarize the situation, thank you for coming, and say that he'll get back to you. You'll then get up, shake hands and leave without knowing where you stand, what the next step will be, when you will be contacted or how.

As you feel yourself being maneuvered into this position, you must again take the initiative to meet your objective. As the interviewer answers your last question, you should lead into the close. Summarize the points you have made so far and the benefits you feel that you can bring to the organization. List the criteria that the prospective employer enumerated early in the interview, and show how your background meets each one.

Then you must ask for some commitment that will achieve the objective that you have set for this interview. If your objective was to be asked back for another interview, make sure this occurs. If your objective was to get a decision on your candidacy, do it now. You must end the interview with some commitment to take a positive next step in the process and to achieve the objective you set.

When to ask for commitment.

As you continue to ask your questions and convince the interviewer to sell himself on you, watch for "buying signals." These are gestures and/or words that indicate a generally positive reaction to your presentation and benefits. Listen and watch for these vocal and visual signs of interest on the interviewer's part. A buying signal can simply be a statement that the interviewer is interested in you and would like to have you come back again. Similarly, the interviewer's reference to the position as "your" job instead of "the" job could be a buying signal.

A sign of interest can be as subtle as a general feeling of relaxation (indicated by body language or increased smiling) or perhaps an offer to tour the facility. It could even be a change in tone that is more informal and relaxed. It's also time to "ask for the order" when you hear words such as the following:

> *I think we could use someone with your skills.*
>
> *Your talents closely match the qualifications sought this position.*
>
> *Well, I'm satisfied. What do you think?*

Buying signals can occur at any time during the interview. But make sure you have established value for your services before asking for the job. Get agreement on several benefits before you summarize and ask a committing question. Think of asking for the job as you would ask someone to marry you. If you're not sure what the answer will be, keep adding more benefits and "reasons to buy" before you pop the question.

If the end of the interview arrives and you're not sure whether or not to ask a committing question, it's better to ask than not to. If nothing else, you're demonstrating your interest in the position, and you will more likely move closer to the attainment of your objective.

How to ask for commitment.

The first step in asking for commitment is to summarize the situation as it appears to you. Relate your benefits to the needs of the interviewer and the company and get the interviewer's agreement on each. The second step is to ask a question. This may sound obvious, but too many people simply make a statement to which a response is not required. For example, if you want to work for a company, a committing question would be "When can I start?" A statement such as "I would really like to have this job" does not ask the interviewer to say that it is yours.

There are two ways to ask for confirmation of your objective: directly asking for a commitment and then indirectly responding to a neutral or negative response. Begin by asking a direct, focusing question that requests some commitment, eliciting either a positive, neutral or negative response. If the answer is positive, you need only agree upon the details (starting day, time, salary, etc.). If the answer is neutral or negative, you have to use other, indirect techniques that will help you find out why the interviewer is not in favor of hiring you. It may be that he just doesn't have enough information or there may be some area of misunderstanding. In either case, you must clarify the issue to his satisfaction. Get him to "sell himself and stay that way."

1) Directly asking for commitment.

Direct questions simply ask for the job. You could phrase it as a closed-response question, seeking a choice between two positive alternatives. Once you ask a direct question, don't say another word. Wait for the interviewer to say something. If you interject some qualifying statement, or another question, you've let him "off the hook." Once you ask for the job, confidently sit back and wait for the answer. Here are examples of direct committing questions:

Should I start work next Monday, or would the 15th be better?

I agree that you could use someone with my skills. Do you want me to start applying them next Monday?

When can I start?

2) Indirectly responding to neutral or negative responses.

If the interviewer does not answer with a positive response, you have to find out why. If he says he needs to know more about you, he probably just doesn't have enough information upon which to base his decision. It's not necessarily an objection, just a request for more information. Find out what areas he would like to know more about; then take your presentation in that direction. Follow your presentation with a clarifying question ("Is that all you needed to know about that?"); then ask another direct question to get commitment.

But if the interviewer seems to be hesitant to say why he will not give you an affirmative answer, you need to apply other, indirect techniques to find out why. Then you can clarify the misunderstanding or handle the objection.

Indirect techniques.

1) The Switch. When using this method, you respond to a negative answer with another question. Get his commitment that the job is yours if you can demonstrate you have the qualification that he doubts. An example of this technique is the following:

Interviewer: *I think you'd probably make a good employee, but I'm just not sure you have enough experience.*

You: *If I can demonstrate to your satisfaction that I can successfully perform in this position, may I have the job?*

OR,

Interviewer: *If I could only find someone with your education but with some retail experience, I would hire her immediately.*

You: *(Assuming you haven't yet told him about your part-time job in retailing during school) Then you're saying that if I had some retailing experience you would hire me?*

2) Dual Questions. With this technique, you ask two questions in a row. The first is a major question, the second, a minor one. The idea is to get the interviewer to agree to the minor question, thereby implying agreement to the major question:

I think we've agreed that I'm perfect for the position. Should I start Monday? And will I still be able to continue my education?

An excellent twist to this method obtains a commitment to proceed no matter which question is answered: "Have you convinced yourself to hire me, or should I tell you more?"

3) The Ben Franklin Technique. An excellent closing method that you can use under almost any circumstances and is perfect for comparing decision criteria and eventually forcing a choice is called the Ben Franklin Technique. You can use it as a logical approach to solving any problem. It is simply a list of all the reasons for going ahead with a decision and all the reasons against doing so. The list with the greater number of items is chosen as the answer.

Before using this technique, you must get the interviewer's commitment that the longest list will decide whether or not you are hired. Take out a piece of paper and set up a chart identical to your Self-Analysis Balance Sheet. Label the left column "Reasons For Hiring Me" and the right column "Reasons Against Hiring Me"

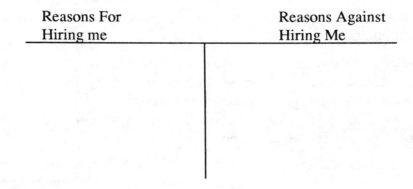

Reasons For
Hiring me

Reasons Against
Hiring Me

Then summarize all the benefits you have presented so far, and list each in the column on the left as you mention it. Keep your Self-Analysis Balance Sheet in mind for ideas to add to the list. Solicit the interviewer's help for thinking of all the benefits you could bring to the position. Then write them down as he says them.

Once you have exhausted the list, turn the pad over to him and ask him to list the reasons <u>against</u> hiring you. Obviously, you won't contribute anything to this list. If he writes down one or two, use the Home-Buyer's technique for minimizing them. Close the "sale" by reminding him of his agreement to implement the decision with the most items in its favor, which will most likely be the column on the left.

4) The Negative Yes. This technique is particularly useful when the interviewer is not willing to divulge his true objection. You simply ask a question, the answer to which is most likely to be "no." But every time the interviewer says "no," his response can be taken as a "yes" if the question is phrased properly.

For example, on the first interview your objective is to be asked back to meet the other decision makers. Your closing statement should be phrased to get a definite time and date to return for the second interview. If the person will not commit to a second interview, you should handle it as an objection. Use your skills to find out why he won't ask you back:

Mr. Jones, I feel good about our discussion today, and I am confident that I could make a valuable contribution to the company. I understand that you have several other people to interview, but I would like to schedule another time to see you. I have a few ideas I need to develop before presenting them to you. I think I could have these ready by next Tuesday morning. Would 9:00 fit into your schedule, or would 11:00 be better?

No. I don't think that will be necessary. I'll review the points we talked about today and call you later.

I can appreciate that Mr. Jones. But just to clarify my thinking, what is it that you want to think over? Is it anything to do with my educational background? ("No.") Does it have anything to do with my summer job at the factory? ("No.") Then does it have anything to do with the salary I have requested? ("Well, it is a little higher than I had wanted to pay for this position.")

Then you proceed to handle it as you would any other objection regarding your salary by breaking it down into smaller increments such as the $2.40 per hour, or any other way with which you feel comfortable.

5) The Call-Back Method. If the interviewer remains firm that you telephone him at some particular time in the future for his decision, you'll have to abide by his wishes. But when you do, there is a technique to use that should make you more successful. When you call back later, don't immediately ask if he has made up his mind. If he is having a bad day or forgets for a moment who you are, he may just say, "No, we won't be hiring you."

Try the following instead. When you get him on the telephone, remind him that he asked you to call back at this time. Then ask if it is a good time to talk. Don't immediately ask for his decision, but try to bring up something you "forgot" to say during your last interview that could be important. Tell him what it is, summarize all your benefits upon which you and he previously agreed, then ask a direct committing question.

You'll have to decide when to stop pressing for commitment. If you sense the interviewer is becoming annoyed at your insistence, back off and accept the situation as it stands. Demonstrate not only your persistence and interest in the position but also your common sense and intuitive skills.

Listening.

One of the most critical factors leading to success in asking committing questions is <u>listening</u> to the answer. Mastering the skill of listening will make more difference in your interviewing success than almost anything else you can do. Effective listening entails understanding and evaluating what you hear and then responding to it.

Many barriers interfere with listening. One is your lack of attention. The interviewer may be talking about something that is of no current interest to you. Your mind may begin to wander searching for a new subject to discuss. Then all of a sudden the interviewer may say something to get your attention, such as "... and if you can do that, I'll give you a bonus of 100% of your salary. Can you do it?" What do you say? Do you tell her that you weren't listening to something that could possibly double your income?

If the interviewer begins to talk about a topic you feel is irrelevant, you have to force yourself to listen. Periodically, make a notation on your pad that will focus your mind on what he is saying. Think of ways you can apply the information to the potential job. Think of questions to ask that demonstrate that you were listening.

Actively listen.

It's important to listen with your body as well as your mind. Nod your head in agreement as the interviewer is speaking (if in fact you do agree with him). Raise your eyebrows briefly if you need to question something that was said without interrupting. Control your eye communication. Use brief assertions of interest to show you are listening. Comments such as "Oh, really?" or "That's interesting." will indicate to the interviewer that you are concentrating on what is being said and that you understand.

Never interrupt the interviewer to change the subject. Similarly, if the person begins talking about a subject you have heard about previously, don't say, "Yeah, I've heard all about that before." Try to move the conversation diplomatically toward a more pertinent subject. If you can't do this, listen actively for comments that you can use to re-direct the conversation politely. Force yourself to listen actively until you get the chance to do this. Practice being a better listener and your career search will be more effective and probably a great deal shorter.

All good things must come to an end.

When it's time to go, the interviewer will normally escort you to the lobby or assign someone else to take you there. In either case, cordially shake hands, thank the interviewer for his or her time and consideration, indicate your interest in proceeding (if it's truly the case) and leave.

Always send thank-you notes.

One of the best ways to differentiate yourself from your competition is to send a handwritten thank-you note to the interviewer and everyone else to whom you were introduced. Summarize your benefits and tell them how much you enjoyed talking with them. You can use one of your advance cards with your picture on it or you could buy preprinted cards and add a personal, handwritten note to it.

Send thank-you notes to everyone with whom you interviewed or interacted. If the receptionist was especially helpful, telephone her to thank her for her assistance. You could also call the interviewer to offer a verbal thank you, especially if you have another offer pending and you want to hurry this decision along. But a written note adds a permanent reminder that you did say thank you. This is one part of your job search that is difficult to overdo. After one period of unemployment I even sent a note to the Director of the Department of Labor to thank him and his staff for always sending my unemployment checks on time.

ASSIGNMENTS:

10.1 Make up a sample Ben Franklin format using the points you listed on your Self-Analysis Balance Sheet. If the interviewer listed any of your weaknesses as a reason not to hire you, what would you say to change his mind?

10.2 With your criteria for an employer and your perfect job description in mind, what questions could you ask an interviewer?

CHAPTER ELEVEN

What's Going Right (and Wrong) With Your Job Search?

A job search can take months to complete. In some cases, it could take a year or more. The causes of the time difference are numerous, but most are under your control. You could perform every activity presented in Job Search 101 but still not experience quick results if your planning or implementation was ineffective.

There is a difference between the terms "activity" and "accomplishment." If you work hard (activity) but are not experiencing a sense of accomplishment, perhaps something is wrong with what you're doing or the way in which you're doing it.

Why perform regular evaluation?

Regular evaluation is necessary to measure your progress against pre-established landmarks. These could be a ratio of job interviews per resume sent, job offers per interview or any other ratios you can create. If you are working hard but not getting results, there is something wrong. You have to find out what it is and correct it.

The best-laid plans...

The research you did or the plan you created may contain problems but more than likely the problem is in implementation. Now you must assess your relative success in achieving your objectives. How are you proceeding toward your goals? Are you getting sufficient quality and quantity of interviews? What is your ratio of second to first interviews? What is going right for you, and what is going wrong? You need to find answers to these questions.

Do your preventive maintenance.

In the evaluation stage, you place your entire job search under scrutiny. This process is not something you do periodically when things are not going well. It should be ongoing and pervasive in order to keep your actions on course. Think of it as preventative maintenance for your career search, something that should be done to prevent problems from occurring.

Re-examine everything, beginning with your goals. Did you make your objective attainable? If you set a target date for getting a job just one month hence, you may have set yourself up for disappointment. Re-evaluate your resume and cover letter. Is your narrowcast letter sufficiently persuasive, and are you sending it to the right people? Have you updated and added to your prospect list and priority system? Are there any "C" prospects that could now be upgraded to an "A" or vice versa?

What should you evaluate?

1) Your cover letter. If you are not generating a sufficient number of interviews as a result of sending out your cover-letter/resume package, these could be in need of repair. First look at your cover letter. Is it persuasively written? Does it impel the reader to review your resume with positive anticipation, or does it simply repeat a series of job descriptions without referring to your accomplishments? Did you follow the AIDA formula?

2) Your resume. It is equally possible that your resume is in need of attention. Is the layout inviting to read? Do you use action-oriented words to present the benefits of your "Potential Product?" Review the checklist in Exhibit 13 to make sure you have adhered to the guidelines. Re-write your resume from a completely different viewpoint just to come up with new ideas. Review the information on creatively re-designing your resume given in Chapter 12. Ask members of your Brain Trust to comment on it again. Call employers who rejected you in the past to solicit their comments on your correspondence. Get feedback from any reliable source, and then revise your resume accordingly.

3) Your prospect list. Your cover-letter/resume package may be well-written and persuasive, but you may not be sending it to the right people. If you have not properly qualified your prospect list, you could be sending your correspondence to suspects who have no need for your services, no matter how good you are. Review your criteria, search for new directories, look for new "A" prospects and try sending your data to other prospective employers.

4) Your interviewing skills. The ratio of second interviews to first interviews is a good indicator of your interviewing skills. If you are receiving a high proportion of first interviews, but are not being offered a chance to come back, the problem may dwell in your interviewing abilities. Go back and review the information in Chapters 8, 9 and 10, and increase your practice time on the fundamentals in each stage.

Assess the organization of your presentation. Are you flexible enough to utilize the right pattern for a given situation? Are you actively participating in the interview? Are you properly asking and answering questions? What about your attitude, posture, greeting and appearance? What else can you do to improve your performance while on an interview?

5) Your attitude. A positive attitude can be one of your greatest assets during your career search. And a negative attitude could be your most bitter enemy. As your search proceeds and the rejection letters keep arriving in your mailbox, your positive attitude may easily slip.

You must continue to believe that if you keep on performing all the activities that are working for you, everything will eventually work out for the best. If you keep trying different approaches, practicing your interviewing techniques, evaluating your responses to questions, sending out more letters, the odds in your favor are much greater. You must keep thinking about what is going right in your search and your life at the present time and do more of it. Make up a new list of tactics and every day think of twenty more ways to implement them. Re-think all your activities, but don't allow your self-confidence to erode to the point that it begins to hinder your activities.

How to perform your evaluation.
Your evaluation process can be both formal and informal. Examples of formal evaluation would be the exit interview and personality or career tests. Informal evaluation could be as simple as asking your spouse or friends, "How am I doing?" Other sources are role-modelling, going to support groups or creating and using a checklist.

1) Formal evaluation.

The <u>exit interview</u> is one that occurs as you are leaving a company or your school. Its purpose is to provide both parties with candid and objective feedback to help the other perform better in the future. Before you leave a company or college, ask your supervisor or teachers to discuss your strengths and weaknesses from their perspective. They usually have nothing to lose by being objective, and some of their comments may surprise you. Ask them what you could have done differently or better. Ask them to list your strengths and weaknesses by creating a Self-Analysis Balance Sheet together.

<u>Career counselors</u> at your college can be helpful. They can offer assistance and consultation on a wide variety of subjects, including vocational opportunities, interviewing techniques and suggestions on how to write or improve your resume and cover letter.

Similarly, there are <u>professional career counselors</u> who, for a fee, will provide many of those same services. These people can also administer personality tests to determine your best career direction. The results of these could be of tremendous assistance to you during your preliminary investigation stages.

2) Informal evaluation.

An informal source of feedback is your <u>spouse/significant other</u>. He or she has a greater understanding of your abilities and desires than others but should be looked upon as a source of <u>subjective</u> information. If your attitude is slipping or you're beginning to sleep later and start the cocktail hour a little earlier each day, he or she can be very helpful by pointing your laxity out to you. But he or she may not want to discuss your character flaws and deficiencies regularly.

<u>Role-modelling</u> can also be helpful. If you talk to people who were successful when they were in your situation, you can ask them what they did to get a job. Ask them to describe their interviewing skills, techniques for writing their correspondence, places to look for prospects and any other suggestions that might help you. Try to follow the directions of those who have already succeeded rather than re-invent the wheel.

If you decide to start your own business, talk with people who have successfully started and built their own businesses. If you decide to purchase a franchise, talk with those who have successfully done that, and learn from them. Find out what they would do over again and what they wouldn't. What would they do more of that worked well? Pick their brain for as much information as you can and build their successes into your plan.

If you are unemployed, consider local <u>support groups</u> to talk with those in similar situations. If you find that the meeting turns into a "Why me?" session, leave it to find a more positive group. Support groups may be hosted by churches or other organizations that seek to bring unemployed people together for mutual assistance. The meetings can be helpful for sharing ideas and methods.

All these methods will be more effective if your are frank in your self-analysis. <u>You</u> are the best source of information about your real self. Only <u>you</u> know if your goal is what you want. Only <u>you</u> know what you did wrong on that last job or during a particularly difficult course in school. Review your Talent-Analysis Sheet and your Self-Analysis Balance Sheet. Were you brutally honest with yourself or reluctant to write everything down because you thought someone else might see it? Get to know yourself, and work with your strengths and weaknesses. For example, if you don't like talking on the telephone, place more emphasis on writing letters to people and following up by mail. You'll be spending more time but you'll be more comfortable and subsequently more successful.

Your job search is what you make it.

Create your own personal checklist to help you delve into every area of your career search. Use it when you talk to role-models as you inquire into their success. Ask them how they handled each of the items on your list.

An example of such a checklist is shown in Exhibit 27, which presents a broad list of areas to evaluate. You should customize the list to your situation. Change it to reflect new activities. Write it in your Career Journal and keep it with you so you can review it at every opportunity. Always keep a pen or pencil with you in your car and immediately write down ideas that come to you. Think about how you can improve your situation and what new tactics you could implement. Keep your Career Journal updated, and use it.

EXHIBIT 27: CAREER-PROGRESS CHECKLIST

❑ How can I better present the skills that I possess and the benefits of these skills to the interviewer?

❑ Have I made all the changes to my "product" that I had planned?

❑ Is my attitude sufficiently positive and enthusiastic?

❑ Have I attempted to strengthen all the weaknesses I listed on my Self-Analysis Balance Sheet?

❑ How else can I better utilize the members of my "Brain Trust?"

❑ Have I priced myself properly?

❑ How can I more properly balance my mass- and personal-communication techniques?

❑ Have I listed all my tactics and generated at least twenty ways to accomplish each? What else could I do?

❑ Are all my communications creative, credible, complete, current, convincing, concise and clear?

❑ Does my resume adequately portray my accomplishments? Does it adhere to the rules in the checklist?

❑ Did I use the AIDA formula in my cover letter?

❑ Have I recorded all the contacts I have made and properly followed up with each?

❑ How can I make my narrowcast letter more persuasive?

❑ What else can I do to control my voice during an interview?

❑ Am I properly using my press kit? Does it have the right examples?

❑ How might I improve my telephone script?

❑ Where else can I look for names of suspects to qualify?

❑ Is my objective specific, measurable, attainable, written and motivating?

❑ What other tactics could I perform?

❑ Do I regularly review my Career Journal to re-evaluate all the aspects of my job search?

❑ What other occupations might I consider?

❑ What other role models can I contact for information about how they succeeded?

❑ What other techniques could I use to practice my interviewing skills?

❑ Is there a support group nearby that I could join for more objective information and assistance?

❑ What else can I do in order to be more successful?

Evaluate every interview.
    Exhibit 28 shows a checklist you can use to review your performance after every interview. The more quickly after the interview you do this, the fresher the information will be in your mind. Adapt it to include your own list of questions, based on your individual circumstances. You must evaluate your efforts and determine other ways to improve your performance during the interview.

EXHIBIT 28: POST-INTERVIEW CHECKLIST

❑ Did I properly prepare for this interview, including a review of the company's literature? Did I spend enough time practicing?

❑ What was my objective for this interview? Did I achieve it?

❑ Did I call to confirm the interview beforehand, and did I arrive on time?

❑ Did I scan the office to find something with which to open the interview personally?

❑ How could I have more effectively opened the interview? What other questions, objects or premiums could I have used?

❑ Did I use the interviewer's name frequently enough? Did I pronounce it properly? Did I get a business card to get the proper spelling for my thank-you note?

❑ How can I improve my questioning skills?

❑ Did I discuss the benefits of my skills and my accomplishments?

❏ Did I use reference letters and testimonials effectively?

❏ Did I effectively handle the objections? Which ones have come up often enough that I should anticipate more effective ways to handle them?

❏ In what other ways can I use the READY formula?

❏ How can I improve my skills in asking committing questions?

❏ Which organization pattern did I use to make my presentation?

❏ Was my presentation effective, or would another format have been better in this case?

❏ Did I actively participate in the interview? How can I do better next time?

❏ How should I follow up on this interview? When? To whom should I send a thank-you note?

❏ What is the commitment for the next step?

❏ How did I look? Was my suit clean and pressed? What about my shirt/blouse? Were my shoes shined?

❏ Did I adequately listen to the interviewer, or did I find my mind wandering to what I was going to say next?

❏ What examples of body language did I recognize? How can I improve my skills in detecting signals of interest?

❏ How did I use eye communication, and how can I improve it?

❏ Did I anticipate the questions sufficiently? Which ones gave me trouble answering? How can I do better next time?

❏ Did I ask the right questions and obtain all the information I wanted?

❏ What else can I do to improve my performance on my next interview?

❏ Would I accept this position if offered to me?

Think of the evaluation process as you would a rear-view mirror in a car. You must check it periodically to see where you have been and what the situation is behind you. But if you dwell on it, you won't see where you are going, and you'll end up in an accident. Use your past only to gain control of your future. If you know what you did right, you can do more of it. If you understand what you did improperly, you can correct your actions and perform more successfully next time

After every interview, go through this checklist to evaluate honestly where you went right. Think about what you could do differently next time, and then begin to assess what you did incorrectly. Although it is necessary to critique each interview constructively, don't automatically begin by seeking what you did wrong. It's important to know the good and bad parts of any situation so you can evaluate it with perspective. If you look at both the positive and negative aspects of your performance, you can make necessary corrections before they become disastrous to your career search.

There is an acronym that can help you evaluate your interviews with balance: **PEN**. First look at what is **P**ositive about the situation, and then look at what you can be **E**nthusiastic about. Once you have this viewpoint, look for what is **N**egative about your performance. You don't have to dwell on the negative, but just provide yourself with an accurate picture of the situation. By beginning with the positive, you can focus on the situation more objectively and set yourself up to take the inevitable negative feedback.

Ask yourself the right questions.

If you phrase your questions in a way that is negative ("How could I have been so stupid?"), you'll dwell upon and relive the negative aspects of your actions. But if you re-phrase the question in a positive way ("How can I improve my actions so that I perform better next time?"), you'll focus your thoughts and actions on ways to correct and improve yourself.

If you hear yourself saying, "Why me? Why do I have to be unemployed during the Christmas season of the worst recession year since 1973?" then you are obviously dwelling on the negative environment. Consider the difference between that thought and this statement indicating a more positive frame of mind: "It's a recession year and unemployment is rising rapidly. That means there are more and more people every day in need of employment. I think I'll write a book to help people help themselves get a job, and we'll all be better off." Learn to distinguish between what you can and cannot control. You can't change the direction of the wind, but you can change the way you set your sails.

Properly define the situation.

Don't focus on the problem, focus on the opportunity. I was once approached in a parking lot by a woman who had locked her car door with the keys still in the ignition. She asked if I had a coat hanger to unlock the door. I have done that many times myself and went to help her. Her door locks were the kind that receded into the door, and the coat hanger trick would not work. She began to despair because she defined the problem with the question "How can I unlock this door?"

I, on the other hand, defined the problem with the question "How can I get into the car?" I began thinking of whom we could call for assistance. There were the police (who in retrospect might have been a good option if the woman was trying to steal the car with my unknowing assistance), AAA or even a locksmith. If it had been a car with a small vent window, perhaps she would have considered breaking the glass (a last resort and probably not a viable option, but nonetheless an idea). After reviewing the situation and realizing the futility of using the coat hanger, I checked the other doors of the car and found one to be unlocked. She was aghast and said she would never have thought of trying the other doors. I found the solution because of the way I defined the challenge.

Be creative in finding new ways to achieve your goals. Look back at all the tactics you wrote down in your marketing plan. What else could you do? How can you implement these differently? Perhaps you were so busy responding to ads and sending out narrowcast letters that you forgot to go to a major trade show in your field. If you have not yet created the form to follow up on all the letters you sent out, you could be missing the one opportunity where the recipient of your letter is anxiously awaiting your call. Perhaps he lost your letter and doesn't know how to reach you. You have to plan every action, implement your plan, follow up diligently and evaluate the relative success of every activity you perform.

Chart a new course for yourself and set sail. Try new ideas. Try old ideas in a different way. Ask other people for advice. Find out what works for you and do more of it. Find out what doesn't work, and get rid of it. But never give up. Never, never give up.

ASSIGNMENTS:

11.1 Create a personal Career-Progress Checklist and write it in your Career Journal.

11.2 Review the cover-letter/resume checklist in Chapter Five and see if there is any way to improve your package.

11.3 Which tactics are working for you, and which are not? How do you know for sure?

11.4 Create your personal Post-Interview checklist, write it in your Career Journal and review it after every interview.

11.5 Do you know anybody who recently went through a successful job search? If so, contact him to find new ideas to incorporate into your quest.

CHAPTER TWELVE

Play "20 Questions" to Stimulate Your Creativity.

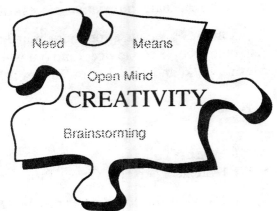

One of the basic guidelines of Job Search 101 is for you to be professionally creative in your planning, implementation and evaluation. This means that if you are to stand out among all your competitors, you must get the attention of the prospective employer in a positive way. You must demonstrate through your actions and words that you are different from and better than all the other candidates for the position.

Creativity is an integral part of this entire process. It allows you to generate ideas that no one else has, and it proves that you will be valuable to have as an employee. A person who can solve problems creatively is prized by a company.

Being creative is not just for those people who do it for a living, such as a writer or artist. Everyone is creative in his own way. Given the need, the means and the open mind, you can come up with ideas to solve your problems. You have the need, since you are looking for a job. This chapter will provide you with the means to generate ideas to implement your search. But only you can provide the open mind.

Job Search 101 is unique because every reading of the book will be different from any previous one. Each time you go through this chapter in particular, you will think of new ways to solve a job-search challenge or implement an idea creatively.

That's the way the ball bounces.

Have you ever watched an inflated ball after you drop it on the ground? Each time it bounces, it doesn't come up as high as the last time and eventually it stops. The same theory applies to your job search. If you don't keep putting the "bounce" back in your search, a bad attitude will pull you down until you stop performing what you must do to succeed. Creativity helps you re-inflate your job search by giving you new ideas to try and new life when you might have otherwise given up.

Stimulate your brain power.

To use this information, you have to learn to "brainstorm" with others or by yourself. Brainstorming is a tactic first applied in a 1950's book by Alex Osborne (Osborne, Alex F., Applied Imagination, Third Revised Edition, Charles Scribner's Sons, NY). The book is old but the theory, like all good ones, remains effective today. In general terms, it states that if you apply four techniques to generate ideas, they will come in greater quantity than you could have imagined. The process will be more successful if you do it with others, i.e., those in your Brain Trust.

The four "rules" are simple. Beginning with a specific objective, you should first attempt to generate a large number of ideas to solve it. At this point, you aren't concerned about how good the ideas are, just that you have many of them. In order to generate many ideas, you should not judge them as they come up, thus the second rule: defer judgement of any comment or idea until later. Your fellow "brainstormers" will cease offering new ideas if they are told that each of their previous ideas was not good. After all the ideas are written down, then you may begin to eliminate those that are of no possible value.

In order for the next rule to be effective, you must "let yourself go" and be as bizarre in your thinking as you can. The third rule is to "freewheel," or to be as outlandish as you can. Think of strange ways to meet the objective of the brainstorming session. These may seem foolish but they may become the spark of a more feasible idea. Therein lies the fourth rule. "Hitchhike" on other comments with an idea of your own. The idea of advertising your availability on a banner towed behind an airplane may be "freewheeling," but following that up with an idea for a "banner" headline across an ad for yourself is an example of "hitchhiking."

RULES OF BRAINSTORMING

1) Quantity vs. Quality

2) Defer Judgement

3) Freewheel

4) Hitchhike

Listed below are twenty examples of techniques you can use to stimulate the flow of ideas during a brainstorming session. The question following each example is designed to activate your thinking in that specific area. Always write down your ideas and thoughts, no matter how disassociated they may seem now, so you have a record of everything that was said.

It's important to have a specific objective in mind when using these creative activators. Write down your goal, and keep it in front of you as you ask yourself each question. You can use these questions as you perform assignment 7.3. Write down the specific tactic you will address that day in the form of a question. Then write the numbers 1 - 20 down the left hand edge. Use the creative stimuli listed here to help you create the twenty ways to implement or address that topic.

1) ASK QUESTIONS OF YOURSELF

The greatest idea-generating questions start with the words "What if..." You then complete the sentence with an idea. This process begins your initial brainstorming activities. Once you get started, the ideas will begin to flow.

Here are some questions you could use to begin to stimulate your thinking. What if...

...you didn't have to work for a living. What would you do with your life?

...you knew you couldn't fail to do something; what would you choose to do?

...there was no such thing as a newspaper. Where would you look for career opportunities?

...you couldn't use a resume to get a job; how would you communicate your credentials?

...there was no such thing as a postal system. How would you deliver your message?

Ask yourself a question in a way that will help you create the greatest possible number of answers. If your question presupposes that there is more than one answer, you will be more likely to think of multiple responses. An excellent technique for using such questions is to begin each with "In how many more ways can I...."

- find existing job opportunities?

- create job opportunities?

- create a better impression during an interview?

- improve my eye communication, grammar, posture, etc.?

> In how many other ways can you solve the challenge facing you now, and what if none of those worked?

2) REPHRASE THE QUESTIONS YOU ASK YOURSELF

As you have seen, the way you ask yourself a question will direct your mind to think of more ways to answer it. By feeding your mind with a positive interpretation of the situation, you are more likely to freewheel successfully.

For example, you could begin by saying, "Why can't I get a job?" Or you could begin with a larger, more positive frame of reference by asking, "What can I do to keep from being unemployed?" The second question could elicit such responses as the following:

Buy a company
Start a company
Work for the unemployment office
Join the military
Get a part-time job while I continue my education

If you hitchhike off one of these, you could increase the quantity of your ideas. For example, "Work for the unemployment office" could spur your thinking along these lines: you could work for your state's unemployment office, your college's Career Placement Department, any college's Career Placement Department, a private personnel agency, the personnel department in a company, etc.

Change your questions to stimulate the broadest number of ideas possible, and then go back to each, using it as a springboard for more opportunities. But you must start with the right questions. Don't ask yourself, "Why can't I write a good resume?" Ask instead, "How can I convince a company to interview me?" Not "Why can't I write better letters" but "In how many ways can I improve my communications?"

> How can you improve the questions you ask yourself to stimulate a positive response for the largest number of ideas?

3) CHANGE THE WORDS

Just as you can stimulate your thinking by rephrasing a question, you can create other ideas simply by changing the definition of one key word to broaden the alternatives it covers.

For example, if you have always wanted to be employed as an artist, you may have searched for opportunities with tunnel vision, seeking only those careers listed under the term "Artist." But in what other careers could you apply your artistic skills? If you changed the word from "artist" to "creative," you could increase your career options to include the following:

- Working for an ad agency
- Serving as a free-lance designer or illustrator
- Becoming a commercial artist
- Drawing cartoons
- Painting scenes on vans
- Creating package designs

Similarly, what if you changed the profession of selling and called it by its generic function. Instead of a "sales person" you could become a "persuader." In what other career directions could you then go? Perhaps you could look into becoming a

• Politician	• Fund Raiser
• Trial lawyer	• Preacher
• Professional Lobbyist	• Teacher

It often doesn't take a major change to create a new image. Think of a kaleidoscope. With one quick movement, you can disrupt the existing pattern and create a completely new image. Just change "something," and see what it does to your outlook in your job search. For example, think about the term "job search" itself. Over the years, the word "job" has taken on a negative connotation as something at which one toils from "9 to 5." How might your creativity be jolted if you called it an "opportunity journey, vocation quest, interview challenge, employment search or even career trek?"

> What one word have you used to define yourself in the past? How could you change it to broaden your areas of opportunity?

4) CREATE A "BIG PICTURE" MENTALITY

Force yourself to look at a broader definition of your efforts. You aren't just applying for a job; you're taking your next step on a lifetime career path. Similarly, your cover letter should be written to get the reader interested in reading your resume, which should be written to get the reader to invite you for an interview resulting in a job offer.

Rarely do events occur without any long-term repercussions. Once you look at the overall scheme of events, the concept of creating a plan becomes more meaningful. You're not just creating a job search plan; you're creating part of a life-long strategy that will maximize your chances of getting what you want out of your life.

You'll find that this "big picture" mentality will help you place each interview in a better perspective, which could in turn help you relax more. Try this technique when you find yourself tensing up before an interview: close your eyes and picture yourself in the nose cone of a rocket. As it takes off, keep looking down and watch the building getting smaller, then the block, then the city, state, country and finally the world. From this viewpoint, your interview won't seem so important.

> What can you do to view your current job search from the perspective of a long-term life plan?

5) USE ANALOGIES TO FORM NEW APPROACHES

Sometimes it helps to clarify an abstract idea in your mind by explaining it in terms of something that is more familiar to you. For example, if you are still uncertain about how to incorporate your current job search in your long-term strategy, it might help to make an analogy of your search with some other concept.

What if your job search was like trying to get an airplane off the ground. First, the pilot locates the destination and creates a flight plan to get the plane and its passengers there quickly and safely. He goes through a checklist to make sure everything is ready for takeoff and corrects any problems. As he is about to take off, he pushes the throttle completely forward for full power, and once airborne he reduces the power to remain flying. Although he cannot see the destination for 99% of the way, he continuously checks landmarks along the way to make sure he is heading in the right direction and makes changes as necessary.

> What analogies can you use to help yourself understand your job-search situation better?

6) TRADE PLACES

Similar to the idea of making analogies is the concept of mentally trading places with someone or something in order to see yourself from a different perspective. Using your imagination in this process will be rewarding.

For example, suppose you are asked to return for a second interview. Since you now know the person, what if you mentally traded places with her as you prepare yourself for the meeting? If you were that person, what would "you" ask you? What would "you" think of your appearance? What would "you" say about your resume and cover letter? And what advice would "you" give yourself about interviewing more effectively, your appearance and your correspondence?

For a twist on this subject, think about great historical figures you admire and ask yourself what they would do to help you. How would Napoleon address the situation? Thus you might think in terms of a "frontal attack" or flanking your "enemy" or continuing your attack until they "surrender and offer you the job."

What would Albert Einstein do? Or Vince Lombardi? One might try to create a formula for success, while the other might motivate you to develop a new "game plan" for each contest. What ideas do you think they would devise to solve your problem? How might they look at your situation differently?

> With whom could you trade places to change your viewpoint and see yourself from a different perspective?

7) CREATE ACRONYMS TO HELP YOU REMEMBER THOUGHTS

An acronym is a word formed from the initial letters of other words. You've already been introduced to several of these. Think back to the BRIAN formula for effective writing and the SALARY acronym for more effective speaking. You also saw how to be READY to handle objections.

Acronyms can quickly remind you to follow certain concepts without having to go back and remember a long list. The reminder will give you the basic concepts immediately, and the other ideas should follow.

Make up your own acronyms to help you write a better resume. You could start with this:

> **R** esults-oriented
>
> **E** asy to read
>
> **S** upport your statements
>
> **U** - oriented (You, being the reader)
>
> **M** issing words or spelling errors?
>
> **E** nthusiastic statements

> What acronyms could you make with the words RELAX, INTERVIEW or BEN-EFIT? What other acronyms can you create?

8) IF IT'S NOT BROKEN, DON'T FIX IT

Make sure you are applying your creativity to the right problem. If you are not generating a sufficient number of interviews, one or more things might be wrong: your resume, cover letter, prospecting list or any combination of them. Through your evaluation steps in Chapter Eleven, decide exactly what parts of your plan need to be revised, and then work on improving those.

You could have a perfectly good resume but if you are sending it to the wrong people, they will not call you for an interview. Conversely, your prospect list could be right on target with all "A" contacts, but if you are sending them a poor cover-letter/resume package, they won't call you for an interview.

> In what ways could you correct a situation where you are sending out letters but not generating interviews? What could be wrong if you are going on many more first interviews than second interviews?

9) FLEX YOUR CREATIVITY

Make it a game to practice using your creativity. As you are driving, look at bumper stickers and try to create jobs from them. For example if you see one that says "I ♥ to Ski," you could think about different jobs relating to skiing. You could be an instructor, buy or start a ski resort, make new skis or become an Olympic skier. What about designing or selling indoor skiing devices to use during the summer. Or maybe the bumper sticker applies to water skiing. If so, you could make or sell boats, outboard engines or water skis.

The next time someone is driving you around, look at license plates, billboards, signs on trucks or anywhere you might see something that would stimulate your imagination. Then apply your imagination to furthering your job search.

> In what other ways could you practice being creative?

10) BEGIN JUST BY DOING SOMETHING.

As you begin to write your correspondence, you may experience "writer's block," a mental block that keeps you from being creative. You can get around it by just starting. Write something, and then change it if necessary. If you just start writing, words will begin to come to you. Set a timer for five or ten minutes and "free-write" about whatever comes to your mind. Don't stop writing until the timer sounds.

Break your objective down into sub-categories. Don't think about writing your entire resume; think in terms of writing only about your experience. Then you can start with your first job and write about it. Once you begin, you can add to or subtract from it to create something different.

Similarly, if you're not sure where to prospect, start somewhere. Go to the library and ask for a directory of companies in your industry or state. If you're not sure how to price yourself, check with your college's Career-Development Center, alumni, personnel agents or just read the papers to see what is being offered to people in similar positions in your industry. If you're ever in a position of not knowing how to start, just do something and then add to it, change it, etc.

> What have you been putting off that you could start right now?

11) KNOW THE RULES

If you know the rules of a job search, you'll be in a better position to judge the intent of the rules. If you allow your creativity to flourish within these intentions, you can keep it within the bounds of professionalism.

For example, the intention of a resume is to communicate the skills and education you have developed and the benefits that these can provide the employer. Its objective is to get you in for an interview. From your reading of Chapter Five, you know at least two general resume formats. These are the functional format and the reverse-chronological format. If you COMBINE these, you could create a resume that looked like that shown below. It is informational and professional, yet slightly different.

EXPERIENCE

       Skill: Creative Problem Solving
          ABC Company   4/3/85 - Present
          Title: job description; specific accomplishments from implementing your creative problem-solving skills

       Skill: Strategic Planning
          DEF Company   8/1/82 -4/3/85
          Title: job description; specific achievements that resulted from your strategic planning

---

As you can see, the intention of a professional, results-oriented resume remains intact. You have just combined two known concepts into your own presentation.

Other ways you could act in a situation without breaking the rules include the following:

- Ask to interview with the people who will be working for you.

- Ask to interview with the president of the company.

- Invite the interviewer and spouse out to dinner (an effective way to get your spouse involved in the decision and your career).

- Instead of going where the jobs are, go where they aren't and create your own.

- Invite the interviewer to a "neutral" place for the meeting (a restaurant, for example, or the exhibitors' lounge at a trade show).

- Start the interview off by asking a question about the company.

In what other ways can you work within the rules to be more professionally creative?

12) DON'T MAKE IT HAPPEN, LET IT HAPPEN.

You'll find you will be most creative when you are relaxed and not under pressure to find a solution to a situation. Some people are more creative in the morning and others in the evening. You'll find that you are more likely to find new ideas while you are playing golf or driving your car long distances. Whenever or wherever it is, go there at that time and create new ideas for your career trek.

Begin by inundating yourself with information. Read Job Search 101 several times and complete all the assignments. Then once you have all the information in your mind, go to your "private place" and "let it happen." Bring this chapter with you to activate your creativity and you'll find that ideas will begin to "percolate" in rapid order.

Where and when do you find yourself to be most creative?

---

13) FORCE YOURSELF TO BE CREATIVE

This may sound as if it's the opposite of point number 12, and it is. But there are times when you need to get started and your "writer's block" just won't go away. Even in your private, creative place, the ideas may not begin to flow, so you need a way to get them started.

You can do this by creating two lists of known facts or concepts and forcing them into combinations that you hadn't thought of before. You can write one list down the left-hand side of a page and another across the top of the page, thus forming the matrix to force new combinations of items.

For example, assume you wanted to find new ways to get your message across to prospective employers in different stages of the job-search process. Perhaps you have already talked to some companies, and you need to remind them that you are still interested. But you've called them so many times that you feel awkward using the telephone again. Or perhaps you want to introduce yourself to others, but you want to use a unique technique when doing so.

To force yourself to think of new ways to accomplish these goals, make a list of the media down the left-hand column and the intent of the message across the top. Then as you go down the "Introduction" column, stop at each medium to think about how you could use it or a variation of it to achieve your objective.

Thus you will force yourself to think of ways to send your career card to introduce yourself or attend a trade show where a prospective employer is exhibiting. Or you could create your own video and send it to a target company via overnight mail.

By changing the axes, you could use the same matrix to force yourself to think of new careers, places to look for prospects, interviewing techniques, job-search activities and new ways to think of new ways. The opportunities for using this system are limited only by your ability to think of ways to use it.

	Introduce	Remind	Inform	Promote	Announce
Resume					
Cover letter					
Reply Card					
Career Card					
Trade Show					
Job Fair					
Billboard					
Bumper Sticker					
Match Books					
Video					
Audio					
Flip Chart					
Press Kit					
Testimonials					
References					
Brain Trust					
Trade Journals					
FAX					
Overnight Mail					
Personal ad					

> What's the biggest stumbling block in your job-search path right now? How can you use this matrix to find a creative way around it?

14) DON'T OVERLOOK THE OBVIOUS

You may get so caught up with trying to find a creative solution to a situation that you forget to look for an obvious answer. Sometimes it is right in front of you, or it may just require a slight twist from your present technique. Here are a few ideas to stimulate your search for obvious opportunities:

- Work at your college after graduation. Why not in the Career-Development office? What about teaching? Or recruiting?

- If you know you're about to be laid off, take the initiative and find a new opportunity that would make the company want to keep you as an employee.

- Start an employment agency. One person who went bankrupt started a consulting firm to help others prevent personal bankruptcy.

- If you are being laid off after several years of working, go back to your alma mater's Career-Development Center for assistance. Many offer a lifetime service for their alumni.

- Look for part-time, temporary or volunteer work in your field to continue making contacts.

- Start a networking or support group.

• Offer to serve as a consultant to the company that is laying you off.

Keep active and keep looking. Don't forget to look in your "own back yard" as Dorothy said in <u>The Wizard of Oz</u>. The answer to your situation may be closer than you think.

What obvious solution might you have overlooked?

---

15) KEEP YOUR EYE ON THE NEXT STEP

An axiom that applies to the way you dress while on the job is "Don't dress for the job you have, dress for the job you want." If all your colleagues wear short sleeved, off-white shirts and sport coats while all those at the level to which you aspire are wearing long sleeved white shirts and suits, you'd better dress as they do.

You can apply this to your job search also. When you are asking questions during an interview, you will obviously ask about the current opportunity. But also ask about where it will lead. What career paths would begin with this position? What next steps will occur, and in what approximate time frame (assuming adequate performance on the job)?

If you apply for a part-time position, follow the same rules as you would for a full-time job. For example, always bring a resume with you on the interview. Many people think that a part-time position is a short-term, dead-end spot that will be terminated as soon as sales get better for the company. This is not always the case. You could look at a part-time job as your chance to show them what you can do. Always look to the next step on your career ladder, and act as if you belong there. Sooner or later you will.

Whether you are in a full- or part-time position, once you complete any assignment, take a moment to look it over carefully and ask yourself, "Is this the best that I can do? Am I proud to show this to someone as an example of the work which I am capable of performing?" If your answer to this question is "Yes," then turn it in and ask , "What can I do next?" If your answer to the previous question is "No," then go back and improve it to the point where you will be proud to sign your name to it.

How can you change your job-search skills to demonstrate to an interviewer that you are interested in moving ahead?

---

16) CHECK YOUR TIMING

Career success can be as simple as being in the right place at the right time. So if you are in the right place at the wrong time, you may not achieve your objective. You can effectively implement all the job-search activities in <u>Job Search 101</u>, create the greatest ideas for getting a job and still not be successful if your timing is not right.

As you perform the research about your product, place, price and promotion, think about your credentials vis-a-vis the current economy. Mid 1991 does not present a great opportunity to begin a career in banking in New England. Nor is it a good time to begin a career selling real estate or automobiles. Undoubtedly these industries will return to their previous levels, but now may not be the time to start a career in them. You might better serve your long-term goals by returning to school for a graduate degree in your specialty. Or if you have a graduate degree, perhaps more specialized training would behoove you.

As with other rules, there are exceptions to this one. If you have all the right tools in place, you could start out on your career trek even during a recession. Since you have to do something, why not do what you like to do? The caveat is to investigate and be aware of the timing of your venture. Use this awareness to your advantage. You also may not have any choice. If you have been laid off and need to find employment, there's no time like the present to begin doing it. The timing may not be the best for your physical location, but perhaps it is better in some other part of the country.

> Is this the best time to begin your search? What else could you do in the meantime to prepare yourself better for future opportunities?

17) CHANGE WITH THE TIMES

No matter how good or bad the timing is now, you can be sure of one thing. It will change. And in order for you to succeed in your career, you'll have to change with it. You have to think and act in today's terms, not yesterday's. If you sought a job five years ago, those same tactics may not be valid now. Similarly, what you didn't do in your search five years ago may be valid now.

How have fashions changed? If you're wearing an out-of-date suit to an interview, you may unfairly be labeled as a person who is not "with it." What about hair styles? Is yours from the '70s or today? Don't forget to update your vocabulary. Not just in your field, but in general.

Begin this job search with an updated self-image. During your last quest, you may have had notions that were correct then but are incorrect now. For example, you may have told yourself before that you were too young or too inexperienced. Now you are five (or whatever number) years older, with that many years of additional experience. Any time you hear yourself saying "I'm too...," you have to be careful. Whatever it is, you have to decide if it is still valid, if it ever was to begin with.

If you have just been laid off, you could be competing with recent college graduates for positions in the marketplace. Have you kept up with changes in your field so that you can compete with them at the same level? Do you need to go back to evening college and become more familiar with the current techniques and terminology in your field? If so, do it.

> What else can you do to make your current job search reflect your understanding of yourself and your environment as it really is today, not as it was the last time you looked?

18) FOLLOW YOUR GUT FEELINGS

When you are in certain situations, you may get the feeling that "something is not right." You can't always pinpoint it, but you can just sense that something is amiss. These same feelings will occur during your job search, and you should "listen" to them.

- If something doesn't feel right about the company or the offer, ask more questions until you uncover the culprit.

- When creating your correspondence, don't use a word or phrase if it seems to bother you. If you aren't sure whether your humorous statement will be taken in the right way, leave it out. If you feel odd calling people by their first names, call them "Mr." or "Ms." until they set a more informal tone.

- As you are deciding which suit to wear, if you feel your tie may be too loud for this company, go with the more conservative outfit.

- If you sense there may be some ulterior motive to an interview question, or if you're not sure of its intent, ask for clarification.

These "hunches" don't always occur in a negative sense. You could just as easily get an intuitive feeling that you should do something positive or that a particular job is the one for you. When you sense a positive feeling, it should motivate you to action.

What hunch do you have now that you should act upon?

---

19) KEEP A POSITIVE PERSPECTIVE

You'll more readily identify and act upon your positive hunches if you maintain a generally positive outlook in your job search. Ideas will flow more freely, and the implementation of each will be more fun if you keep an optimistic frame of mind. Remaining optimistic is not easy, particularly under the circumstances you probably find yourself in now and also because of the negative outlook of many people.

You can find this negative influence in many places. The newspapers talk about 6% unemployment instead of 94% employment. There are even statistics that point out how few jobs are being advertised today vs. years ago. But your inner self-confidence will help you to recognize that less than 25% of the available jobs are advertised. Consequently 75% of the opportunities can be found where your competitors are not looking, certainly improving your chances. You can remain confident that your narrowcasting and other creative activities will help you locate a position when others see only the bleak statistics.

Many times when people come up against a stone wall, they give up and try to find an easier path. If you maintain a positive approach you will think as a great sculptor once thought: "Inside every block of stone there lurks a perfect form." Then, when you reach what others think is a stone wall, you can begin chipping away at it until you form your own opportunity.

> What can you do now to create a positive approach in your job search where you or others once just saw a stone wall?

20) PLAY THE ANGEL'S ADVOCATE

There are certain words and phrases that people use to mask their negative feelings so they appear positive. When you hear these phrases, they should trigger a warning in your mind that your idea is about to be put down. One of these phrases is "Let me play the Devil's Advocate." Then the person begins to point out all the reasons why it won't work.

There are many other words that hide negative feelings but probably none as prevalent as, "If it was such a good idea, someone would have already thought of it." And people who say these words are right. If it is a good idea, it's likely that someone has already thought of it. But it's not as likely that he implemented it, probably because of a Devil's Advocate. The fact that you thought of an idea doesn't make it a good one. You have to put it to use. Find out how it can be improved. Play the Angel's Advocate and find ways to make it work. Only then is it a good idea.

> What good ideas have you had that you didn't put to use because of a Devil's Advocate? What phrases can you use to trigger a warning in your mind?

Conclusion.

You can apply these principles of creativity to your job search in many ways. You can use them to stimulate ideas for planning, implementing and evaluating your activities. The ways you prepare and introduce new tactics in each of these areas will make you stand out professionally and get the job.

Don't think that you're not creative and therefore these techniques could never work for you. Begin just by doing something. Start out with the matrix in point number 13 and then ask yourself "What if..." questions. Then trade places with some of your heroes and view the situation from their perspectives. What does your gut tell you when someone tries to play the Devil's Advocate with your new ideas? Flex your creativity muscle, and you'll be surprised at how well it will work for you. Among other positive results, you'll have more fun in your search.

This chapter makes <u>Job Search 101</u> and your job search unique. Apply your creativity to your specific situation and you will make every reading of this book different from the last. You'll generate ideas you hadn't thought of before, and you'll enjoy the process that much more. Eventually, you'll find just the right combination of events and ideas that will land you that elusive job offer of your dreams.

ASSIGNMENT:

12.1 Take each point listed above and re-read it, one at a time. Think of answers to the question following each; then implement them in your job search.

CHAPTER THIRTEEN

Stop The World, I Want To Get On.

There are many actions you can take in order to get a job. But the most important things you can do are to plan your work, work your plan, and don't give up. At times it may seem as if you are not getting any results and you may get discouraged. Then all of a sudden you'll get a call from a prospective employer. Just keep trying new tactics and implementing them in new ways.

Plan your work and work your plan.

Don't wait until you have the "perfect" plan in place before beginning. There is no perfect plan in a job search. Start with your best plan, take some action and then constantly evaluate and improve your implementation. Keep notes in your Career Journal so if you ever have to go through it again, you'll have a record of all the mistakes you made the first time around.

Take the responsibility upon yourself to get started and see your search through to its successful completion. Instead of saying to yourself "Something must be done about this situation," say, "I have to do something about this situation." Never give up, and remember that "If it's to be, it's up to me."

Take action now.

And you should <u>immediately</u> begin your journey to career success. Don't procrastinate. Commit yourself to doing something at every waking moment to further your quest. Act quickly and positively to create a successful job search and firmly establish these habits for future success. Perhaps one last acronym will help you remember how to take **ACTION**:

<u>A</u>ttitude: Maintain a positive and confident self-image. Let your awareness of your inner worth be reflected in your posture, your words and your actions.

<u>C</u>ommitment: Pledge to yourself that you will do whatever it takes to succeed legally and morally.

<u>T</u>enacity: Don't give up until you have accomplished your goals. Results are achieved by crowding as much purposeful activity into <u>today</u> as possible. Keep doing each next thing in your plan until there are no more next things to do. Then you must create more ideas and implement those.

<u>I</u>deas: Approach every challenge creatively to find a new, professional and innovative idea to meet it.

<u>O</u>pportunity: Look for the opportunity in every situation and dwell on <u>it</u>, not the negative consequences.

<u>N</u>ow: Don't procrastinate. Every positive action has an equal and positive reaction. But no payoff for today's actions will come until some time in the future. If you don't act today, no reward will come tomorrow. Plan your work, work your plan, and do it now.

Take time to smell the roses.

Even with a closely knit Brain Trust to rely upon, you'll find the road to career success a lonely one. All the work you perform goes unnoticed by many people. You'll receive a negative response 99.8% of the time, and you'll never know how close you came to the "final cut" on every one of them. In order to maintain your positive attitude, you have to make your quest as much fun as you can. Find a way to enjoy your activities as much as possible. Reward yourself for the minor successes that will keep you going.

For example, if you enjoy working out at a gym in the morning, you could incorporate part of your job search into your exercise routine. You could take the newspaper into the sauna with a yellow marker, a cup of coffee and a bagel, making that part of your "required reading" as much fun as possible. Then armed with Tuesday's Wall Street Journal or Friday's National Employment Business Weekly, treat yourself to lunch at a local restaurant and review the paper over a hamburger and soft drink. You may come to look forward to these times that help make the most of a less-than-enjoyable situation.

All your work will pay off.

As the time gets close to an offer, think about what you will say when it comes. Review your list of employer criteria. If there is one major item on your list missing in the company, you should reconsider your candidacy. Remember the "Home-Buyer's" technique for handling objections? Just as there is no perfect home, there is no perfect job. You'll have to make trade-offs, but always think twice about doing so with major criteria.

If you are the candidate chosen for the position, you will normally be offered the job in person. When you finally hear the words "I'd like to make you an offer," you will feel an excitement that will be hard to repress. Remain "cool" and listen carefully to what they have to offer.

Unless you are absolutely sure you want the position, it is not necessary to accept it on the spot. Even if you have no other offers to consider, you may want time to think about it or talk it over with your spouse. Or you may need a little more time to check out the company's references. Make sure you are comfortable with all aspects of the offer, the company and the people before you say yes. A bad decision at this time could place you back in the job market a year or two in the future.

Negotiate from a position of strength.

If you have questions about details, now is the time to discuss them. If you have criteria that you "demand," now is the time to negotiate. Once you accept, you lose much of your bargaining power.

For example, you could receive an offer from an out-of-state company that includes a salary figure only. You'll have to ask questions such as what amount of the moving expenses would be covered and whether packing is included in that amount. What about reimbursement for house-hunting trips for your spouse and yourself? And what provisions do they have regarding storing your furniture or financial assistance in buying and selling your house? Get answers to any such questions that bear upon your particular situation before you accept.

You must be careful with your first job out of school. Be sure about every detail of the position, the company and the people with whom you will be working. Make your decision and live with it for as long as you can. If you cannot demonstrate the ability to remain with a company, you will get the reputation of a "job-hopper," making you less marketable to major companies. You may think that one or two quick job changes won't make a difference in the long run, but they will. Find a good job right out of school and stick with it until you have demonstrated your ability to move up in the organization.

Accepting the offer.

If you accept the offer, send a letter of thanks to your supervisor-to-be. Politely summarize your job title, general duties and salary to which you have agreed. Don't write this letter in the form of a contract, but outline everything that was discussed, including your starting date, compensation, training period, commission percentage or bonus amount. If any special arrangements were made, such as use of a company car, document them also. Your supervisor may not be employed at the company when you show up for work. So it's a good idea to have the details of your agreement outlined in this correspondence, especially if you're dealing with a "friend."

This note serves another function. There is a marketing term called "cognitive dissonance," or more generally known as "buyer's remorse." It means that immediately after a purchase, a buyer will begin to question his decision. The greater the amount of the item, the greater this re-assessment will be. Your note to your new employer will help reduce any cognitive dissonance and re-affirm the wisdom of his decision to hire you.

Declining the offer.

If you decline the offer, be equally polite. Don't burn any bridges by telling the company that you never considered taking such a demeaning job as that which they offered you. Don't flaunt your higher paying or higher-titled job in their faces. Simply state that after carefully weighing all the factors, you chose another opportunity. Confirm your decision in writing, and tell them you appreciate their consideration and wish them well in the future.

Rescinded job offers.

One event that is difficult to anticipate is the rescinded job offer, an offer that is revoked before you begin work. If you do all your research on the company, and if you are honest with the interviewer, the likelihood of this happening is remote. On the other hand, the rescinded offer may have nothing to do with the events leading up to your hiring decision. It could be a conclusion reached after you accepted the offer. So keep your options open until you begin working on the job. And if an offer is rescinded, get right back into your search and keep the momentum going.

But once you start working, cut the cord with all the other opportunities you had going for you. Politely tell all the prospective employers that you have accepted another position, and thank them for their interest.

A career is a terrible thing to waste.

There is a story that has circulated around the business world for more than twenty years. Perhaps it will offer incentive for you to evaluate what it is you are doing with your career. It goes something like the following: